PROPHETIC
BATTLE PLAN

DIANE M. NEUMANN

Matthew 5:17 - 18

"Do not think that I came to destroy the Law or the Prophets. I did not come to destroy but to fulfill. For assuredly, I say to you, till heaven and earth pass away, one jot or one tittle will by no means pass from the law till all is fulfilled.

PROPHETIC
BATTLE PLAN

*A*dvantage
BOOKS

HEAVEN'S BATTLE STRATEGIES FOR
ENFORCING CHRIST'S VICTORY ON EARTH

DIANE M. NEUMANN

Prophetic Battle Plan: Heaven's Battle Strategies for Enforcing Christ's Victory on Earth by Diane M. Neumann

Copyright © 2025 by Diane M. Neumann

All Rights Reserved.

ISBN: 978-1-59755-849-5

Published by: ADVANTAGE BOOKS™
Longwood, Florida, USA
www.advbookstore.com

Unless indicated in context of the chapters, Scripture taken from the NEW KING JAMES VERSION®. Copyright© 1982 by Thomas Nelson, Inc. Kindle Edition. Used by permission. All rights reserved.

Library of Congress Catalog Number: 2025947771	
Name:	Neumann, Diane M., Author
Title:	Prophetic Battle Plan: Heaven's Battle Strategies for Enforcing Christ's Victory on Earth by Diane M. Neumann Advantage Books, 2025
Identifiers:	ISBN: Paperback: 9781597558495
Subjects:	RELIGION: Christian Life – Inspirational
	RELIGION: Christian Life – Spiritual Warfare RELIGION: Christian Life – Spiritual Growth

First Printing: October 2025
25 26 27 28 29 30 31 32   10 9 8 7 6 5 4 3 2 1

Table of Contents

Introduction

The body of Christ, His Ekklesia, has entered into a new era. Some call this the Kingdom Era. Others refer to it as the Glory Era. Doctor James Horvath traces its beginnings to 2014. Other prophets claim the Faith Movement of 1980's started the process. During this time, the Holy Spirit has called numerous units of believers in Jesus Christ as Lord of their lives into alignment with God's will for what is now known as the third Great Awakening Movement around the world. Those who have answered this call have been led into new ways of operating within the Ekklesia of Christ. Each person's answer has been dependent on John 14:15

If you love me, keep my commandments.

Yes, it is a test of love. It is beyond simply obeying what is written in the Bible. During this testing time, God has stretched His people to move out of their comfort zones and trust what they do not understand with their natural minds. It requires love grounded in a willingness to walk in faith. After all, faith is trust in the unseen and confidence that God will find a way to bring all results under His authority and plans (Hebrews11:1). The hope is in God alone. It is the action stage of what Jesus further stated in John 14:23 -24

[23]Jesus answered and said to him, "If anyone loves Me, he will keep My word; and My Father will love him, and We will come to him and make Our home with him. [24]He who does not love Me does not keep My words; and the word which you hear is not Mine but the Father's who sent Me."

For those who profess Jesus Christ as Lord and Master of their lives, keeping all the words of scripture is an act of love. It is more than a discussion of the value of the Bible in the modern era. It is more than loyalty to God and His principles. Love implies an intimate relationship with God. When followers of Jesus Christ repent of past thinking, actions, and beliefs and choose Jesus, they enter into a dependency on Jesus Christ and their King above all. This is loyalty. By God's grace, these followers receive positional salvation. In the courts of heaven, they are redeemed and returned to right relationship with God by the blood sacrifice of King Jesus. It is God's intent for this to be a beginning, not an end, in relationship with Him. God intends our gratitude for this salvation will result in seeking Him and His Kingdom. The key to moving forward is to love God above what the world has to offer. It is seeking the beloved in obedience and faith. It is letting go of the need to know the results before following in faith.

The world has been under an onslaught of fear from the enemy of God, particularly from 2019 – 2022. Some people first placed their faith in medicine and government. Others allowed fear to cripple their movements, their interaction with families and friends. Some even attacked those who did not believe in these systems labeling the people as part of the problem. Some turned to God, trusting the words of His Bible before the words of the media. Fear kills trust in God. It breeds double-minded faith. It destroys hope in Creator God as the source and solution to all situations. During this same time, the Holy Spirit was calling His army of believers to pray. Units formed all over the world, lifting up God as the source of the solution. They walked in faith and obedience. As stated in Hebrews 11:6

> *But without faith it is impossible to please Him, for he who comes to God must believe that He is, and that He is a rewarder of those who diligently seek Him.*

They rested on the scripture in 2 Chronicles 7:14.

> *If My people who are called by My name will humble themselves, and pray and seek My face, and turn from their wicked ways, then I will hear from heaven, and will forgive their sin and heal their land.*

These units of believers continued to pray and seek God. Holy Spirit has used these people to form a spiritual army to complete God's plans for the success of the Third Great Awakening around the world. During this time many have received rewards, mantles, tools, directions, and methods to know in their spirits how to operate in this new era. Each has been honed by the righteous fire of God as they moved in faith and love. Surrender and obedience are the coins used to continue in the leading of the Holy Spirit.

I have been blessed to be involved in one such prayer group known as 7:14. We pray every morning on the internet and many different states and nations are part of this group. Though I know and trust Hebrews 11:6, I also had no idea what God was accomplishing in my spirit as I followed where the Holy Spirit was taking me. When I moved in love for God and obedience to His leading, I learned how to rise in my spirit and be a warrior from heaven. God has given me the gift of writing so I may lead others on the same journey. I encourage you to follow the pathway I was shown and enter into powerful prayers as we live thy Kingdom come on earth as it is in third heaven. May all the glory go to our King, Jesus!

1

Creation of Our Bodies by God

God created humanity to possess three related, but different bodies. People are first spiritual beings possessing a spirit body. God first imagined each person in spirit form or what is known in the Bible as inward parts. God molded each individual in their mother's womb through the spirit body to develop a physical body. As stated in the Bible, the spirit form was covered with a physical form. To these two bodies God added a soul that communicates between the other two bodies. The verses in Psalm 139 make it clear it is the soul body that understands or knows these truths. As stated in *Psalms 139:13 – 17:*

> *13For You formed my inward parts; You covered me in my mother's womb. 14I will praise You, for I am fearfully and wonderfully made; Marvelous are Your works, And that my soul knows very well. 15My frame was not hidden from You, When I was made in secret, And skillfully wrought in the lowest parts of the earth.*

First God created each person's inmost being. The Bible is not describing internal organs, but rather a person's spirit. This spiritual body is eternal. Our eternal God, who is spirit, created another spiritual being. The truth about being eternal exists in each person's heart (Ecclesiastes 3:11). The heart referred to in this verse is part of the soul body. Then God placed each spiritual being into their mother's womb to form a physical body. God took the DNA of the mother and combined it with the father's DNA to form a physical body.

The pattern God envisioned for this three-part entity was based on God's own image. As God is three in one, Father God, Jesus Christ the Son, and Holy Spirit, so humanity was created in this three-in-one combination. In Genesis 1: 26a our triune God states:

> *Let Us make man in Our image, according to Our likeness; (Thomas Nelson. NKJV, Holy Bible . Thomas Nelson. Kindle Edition)*

When God talks to all three parts of Himself, He describes making humanity in three interdependent bodies, similar to the Godhead. God is three-in-one, Father God, Jesus Christ the Son, and Holy Spirit. In creating humanity God made one part spirit body, and the second part is a physical body. There is a third part, a mediator of the other two, called a soul body. The physical body deteriorates over time. In death, it is destroyed. The spirit body is eternal. The soul body is also eternal. In Genesis 2:7

God breathed life into Adam's soul body. The Hebrew word, *nepas*, used in this Old Testament verse is translated as *soul* in English. It literally means the act of breathing, or essence of life (Strong's Concordance, 5315). Later in Leviticus 17:11, the power of this soul life is connected more deeply to the blood.

> *For the life of the flesh is in the blood, and I have given it to you upon the altar to make atonement for your souls; for it is the blood that makes atonement for the soul.*

What was breathed into humanity, through God, the essence of life, is stored in the soul, expressed in the blood of people. If this were not so, blood could not be offered for the sins committed by the eternal soul body. They are to be intertwined within each other. This unity of the eternal breath of God, held in the soul body, is captured in the blood that then pours life into the flesh body. The soul is spirit, not physical, or of the earth. Only that which is from the life of God can give life. The interdependent relationship between soul body and physical body is one of many that allows our spirits to exist in the physical world. When a spirit is planted in the womb of the mother, this soul body is encased within the spirit body. The new blood of the child absorbs the soul body. This combination of interacting spirit, soul, and blood in the child, physically grows the child in the mother's womb as the spirit imprints itself on the flesh/soul body combination. Jesus stated in John 3:6

> *"That which is born of the flesh is flesh, and that which is born of the Spirit is spirit."*

What is spirit is eternal and returns from where it came. When a person dies, the spirit body and the soul body, both derived from Father God, return to the source in the spiritual realm. The flesh body decays and returns to earth from where it was created as noted in Psalm 139.

Think and Write about it

The three bodies in a human being are listed below. Name one distinct characteristic for each one.

1. Spirit

2. Flesh

3. Soul

Parts of the Soul Body

In Romans 2:14-15 Paul describes how a soul functions within people whose only spiritual reference is their conscience. The conscience, or sense of righteousness, is the remnant of the restricted spirit body. The conscience is the result of knowing in the soul body both evil and good. Paul's usage in this passage expands one's understanding of the soul as the Hebrew word intends it to represent.

> [14](...*for when Gentiles, who do not have the law, by nature do the things in the law, these, although not having the law, are a law to themselves,* [15]*who show the work of the law written in their hearts, their conscience also bearing witness, and between themselves their thoughts accusing or else excusing them)...*

The three-part nature of the soul is described in verse fifteen. The laws of God and the requirements of the law are written on their hearts. Though these Gentiles have not been taught the Law and its requirements, they use it to govern their actions. It is written on their soul-heart. This soul-heart is the first part of the soul body. Those of the Jewish faith are told to write the laws on their soul-hearts and then meditate on them (Joshua 1:8). As God explained to Joshua, the purpose of meditating and writing the law on the soul-heart was to not stray from the statutes of God. It is how to stay in covenant relationship with God. Covenant with God brings life and blessings into the life of the believer (Joshua 1: 7 – 8). The soul-heart then, is not simply an emotional center, but rather a combination of a thinking structure, personal history, and emotions. All this together is the soul-heart, a source used as a guide for choices and actions. It is a compass to interpret events and impressions happening in a person's life. This is why God tells His people to write His truths of His Words on their soul-hearts. The soul-heart is their standard for judging actions, thoughts, and events. The soul-heart is the foundational beliefs and attitudes of the person. People who have not chosen Jesus Christ as their Lord create this soul-heart by applying:

➢ all their life experiences,

➢ their emotional reactions to the experiences

➢ their interpretation of life events

➢ what other people tell them is true

➢ what those they value have taught them to believe

Until the choice is made to accept Jesus Christ as Lord, all people respond to life within this limited soul-heart. This soul-heart is limited or handicapped because wisdom of both evil and good rest within the soul body. The truth of God accessed through the spirit body is limited. This gives the physical body greater influence within the soul body. Interpretation of life is more focused on the thoughts and experiences from physical senses. The desires of the world have a greater impact.

As noted in 2 Corinthians 4:4

> *...whose minds the god of this age has blinded, who do not believe, lest the light of the gospel of the glory of Christ, who is the image of God, should shine on them.*

In addition to the limited access to the spirit body to know God's will, the enemy has blinded humanity with fear. Fear is the opposite of faith. It is what Adam embraced when the results of rebellion against God's principles manifested in his life (Genesis 3:10). Faith is trusting in what is not seen in the physical world and trusting a relationship with God. Faith is a tool to enter into understanding with the spiritual body. Fear is focusing on what can be lost in the physical world. It embodies loss of life, or death, as well as chaos, punishment, and lack. It drives a person to prefer trusting their own understanding over spiritual revelations. This is what blinds the spirit eyes from knowing God and God's ways. Between desires tantalizing people into focusing on the earthly realm and fear driving them to build their own protection and safety, the enemy of God blinds the eyes of the spirit body and deafens the spiritual ears. These two forces write on the soul-heart forming a reference for choices.

A choice center, or will, uses these truths within the soul-heart as a gauge for judging one's own behavior. This soul-will is a combination of the will and ability to choose. It is a second part of the soul body. It is commonly referred to as the will. It is the part that activates decisions. God gave humanity the ability to reason and choose. It is here a person may choose to submit to God's ordained authority or override it. The enemy uses fear, pain, rejection, and guilt to harden the soul-heart. He also uses desires to control, seek power and prestige, which hardens the soul heart. These are just a few ways in which the enemy twists the will center to subvert the soul-heart to turn from the spirit body that is limited and focus on the physical world.

The third part of the soul body is explained in terms of thoughts. The soul-mind is the one forming thoughts that either support the heart-soul or develop excuses for ignoring it. The soul-mind evaluates the input from the five senses, the history of personal experiences, as well as the words and actions of others. This is the place the enemy tries to bury lies and half-truths in a person. Because the connection to the spirit body is weakened by the knowledge of evil, the flesh body has a greater influence on the soul body. Until one turns their life over to Jesus Christ as Lord, the spirit body has minimal communications with the soul body. This physical body is influenced by the desires of the world. This is what James is describing in James 1:14 – 15:

> *14But each one is tempted when he is drawn away by his own desires and enticed. 15Then, when desire has conceived, it gives birth to sin; and sin, when it is full-grown, brings forth death.*

The standards held within the soul-heart are challenged by the desires within the physical body. These are not simply fleshly desires. They can be drives to be accepted or loved, as well as seeking prestige and control over situations. These are just a few of the desires that entice a person from the earthly realm. The temptations Jesus faced in the wilderness illustrate the scope of these enticing desires. The soul-mind then evaluates and decides whether to honor what is in the soul-heart or activate the desires calling from the earthly world. Paul describes this battle in Romans 7:15 – 17

> *15For what I am doing, I do not understand. For what I will to do, that I do not practice; but what I hate, that I do. 16If, then, I do what I will not to do, I agree with the law that it is good. 17But now, it is no longer I who do it, but sin that dwells in me.*

The battle is within the soul body of the person. Since most information is gained through the physical body, there is an unequal battle within the soul body. The heart-soul is weakened by having very little input from a compromised spirit body. Knowledge of both good and evil writes concepts on the soul-heart. Condemnation and guilt are the products of overriding the soul-heart dedicated to God before a person is reborn in one's spirit. The actions which follow the desires of the physical body birth thoughts of blame, shame, regret, and guilt that are written on the soul-heart. All of these are written on the soul-heart, creating strongholds within the soul-heart. Uncertainty and distrust of self breeds fear. The soul body becomes weighed down. Now these thoughts have power after the original actions were committed. The soul-mind breeds these thoughts recycling accusations, guilt, and shame to continually accuse a person. Sometimes the soul-mind starts rationalizing and justifying the actions in order to repeat them. These thoughts harden the soul-heart. This battling is what both James and Paul are describing within the soul body of a person who does not have a reborn spirit through commitment to Jesus Christ as Lord.

Think and Write about it

Compare and contrast the ways the three parts of the soul operate before and after being reborn in Jesus Christ.

    1. Heart:

2. Will:

3. Mind:

Those who choose to accept Jesus Christ as Lord of their lives have surrendered their soul-wills to God. By inviting Jesus Christ to be Lord of one's life, authority is given to God. Surrender allows us to move back into right relationship with God. God's grace renews the spirit body of the believer. As summarized in Titus 3: 4 – 7:

> *4But when the kindness and the love of God our Savior toward man appeared, 5not by works of righteousness which we have done, but according to His mercy He saved us, through the washing of regeneration and renewing of the Holy Spirit, 6whom He poured out on us abundantly through Jesus Christ our Savior, 7that having been justified by His grace we should become heirs according to the hope of eternal life.*

God, who is love, sent mercy, delaying the results of our actions that were against God's divine order. In this spiritual space created by God, an exchange occurred. Included in the surrender of will was an admission of the guilt of rebellion against God. A choice to leave all this behind or repent was announced in this space. A verbal agreement to make Jesus Christ the Lord of one's life is given. Jesus' death was accepted as payment for every act, thought, desire, and emotional burden carried within our soul bodies. By the grace of God, believers are now in right standing with God. A seed of Spirit is planted in the spirit of the believer that renews the spirit body of the believer. No works by the individual can create this spiritual space of exchange. It is God's lovingkindness that created this spiritual space. In this spiritually created space, God cleansed the soul body within the individual of the pull of evil that had contaminated the person's soul. Accepting the gift through faith is a surrender to the power of the Holy Spirit. A communication between the Holy Spirit and the renewed spirit body of the believer is activated. The renewed spirit body of the individual now relates to the soul-heart. As stated in Ephesians 1:13 -14

> *In Him [Jesus Christ] you also trusted, after you heard the word of truth, the gospel of your salvation; in whom also, having believed, you were sealed with*

the Holy Spirit of promise, [14]who is the guarantee of our inheritance until the redemption of the purchased possession, to the praise of His glory.

In this divinely created space of surrender to Jesus Christ as Lord, the Holy Spirit also sealed the spirit body of the believer to the spirit world. Both the awakened spirit body in the new believer and the connection of the Holy Spirit to the spirit body of the believer is reconciliation. In addition to the seed of spirit planted in the spirit body, the Holy Spirit enters the spirit of the individuals to seal them.

Before accepting Jesus Christ as Lord, all three bodies were not communicating as God intended at creation. By the act of Adam and Eve, all people inherited modified spirit-soul-physical bodies. Paul draws attention to this when explaining the mercy given to all people in Romans 11:30 – 32

> [30]*For as you were once disobedient to God, yet have now obtained mercy through their disobedience, [31]even so these also have now been disobedient, that through the mercy shown you they also may obtain mercy. [32]For God has committed them all to disobedience, that He might have mercy on all.*

As stated earlier in Titus, God's mercy allows people to access the reconciliation through the blood of Jesus. It is God's method of bringing back to His divine order what was His original creation. The spirit body of the believer now has awakened access to the spirit world. This information within the spiritual world can be gathered and submitted to the soul body to evaluate and make decisions. The soul-heart can now re-evaluate core values and beliefs. The soul-mind can be renewed to trust and live by faith and not by works. Since the will is surrendered to God, re-aligning the soul body to God's will is an action the person can now do. Daily surrender of a person's will to God allows the soul body immediate access to the spirit body and the wisdom of God.   It is the hope of the person described in Hebrews 10: 22 – 23:

> [22]*...let us draw near with a true heart in full assurance of faith, having our hearts sprinkled from an evil conscience and our bodies washed with pure water. [23]Let us hold fast the confession of our hope without wavering, for He who promised is faithful.*

Reconciliation through the Blood of Jesus

God intended that both one's spirit body and one's physical body were to interact with one's soul body. The soul body interacts with the physical body interpreting the five senses, making choices, applying what is discerned through the five senses in thoughts and actions. The reborn spirit body also uses spirit body organs to interact with and interpret the spiritual world. The organs within the spirit body were created to function in similar manner to the organs in the physical body. They interpret the spiritual world. These organs are activated through faith.

The original pattern within the three bodies of humanity enabled Adam to communicate directly with God, Spirit-to-spirit. God spent time with Adam teaching him the Kingdom of God principles as illustrated in Genesis 2:15 – 18

> *15Then the LORD God took the man and put him in the garden of Eden to tend and keep it. 16And the LORD God commanded the man, saying, "Of every tree of the garden you may freely eat; 17"but of the tree of the knowledge of good and evil you shall not eat, for in the day that you eat of it you shall surely die."*

Whenever the Bible uses God's title of LORD, the authority of God as King, and ruler of all He created is emphasized. God is instructing His vassal within this earthly kingdom of the rules of order and harmony he is to apply for life to be maintained within the earthly world. The first rule under the authority of God is to tend the garden. So many assignments rest in this verb "tend". Adam was to nurture the growth and development of the garden. He was to cultivate it, noticing the seasons and the various needs of the plants as seasons changed. The needs of plants during the day and during the night are different. Adam was to notice and ponder these things. Questions such as, "How does the day and night cycle keep the life active in the plants?" is just one example of pondering and learning Kingdom of Heaven principles. It is the activity of the second word, *keep,* in the commands from God. Adam's actions towards the plants were to change as the seasons did. He was to notice the rhythms and patterns as the flowers change, becoming fruit and new seed. Through the variety within the garden plants, nuances of life are observed. God's desires for variety were illustrations of his multiple ways of expressing His love in His creation. This was the first level of learning to seek and find God's spiritual wisdom in His creation.

In keeping with God's intent for humanity to have free will, God used the tree of knowledge of good and evil. Every government has rules to protect its people. There are limitations to be respected. Only one plant was denied Adam. In essence, God was saying, "Obey Me in giving back to Me one tree. Learn My ways through tending My garden. Show Me your submission to My authority and remain in My will by giving Me one tree." As in most parent-child relationships with young children, God does not explain in detail the reasons behind this decision. It is for Adam's protection God gives this command. He simply told Adam the results of willful disobedience.

With the creation of animals, another learning opportunity happened for Adam. On the fifth day of creation, living, moving, breeding beings were created to inhabit the earth and seas. God brought these creations to Adam (Genesis 2: 19 – 20). Adam's soul body would apply the spiritual wisdom spiritually discerned as he examined each creature. These creatures had souls which are from the spiritual realm. Just as God spoke them into existence, now Adam was to seek the spiritual word of life buried in each one and call the name based on spiritual truth. Adam was practicing the gift of seeing truth in the spirit and declaring it in the earthly world. Adam was to declare with his mouth, aligning with the spiritual world what God had already ordained within each animal. His mouth was to declare an agreement with God's divine purpose and own it within the earth. This required examining the nature of animals and seeking the differences and variety in each species. In studying animals, a different way of breeding is being taught to Adam. The dependency of the animals on the plant life is seen. The power of agreement with the spiritual word of God to bring order to the relationship between plant life and animal life is learned. The value and power of the spoken word is learned.

Adam's action of choosing to eat the fruit of the forbidden tree within the Garden of Eden was an act of rebellion. Adam knew it was a deliberate breaking of the authority of God over the earthly kingdom. Both Adam and Eve chose to disregard God's requirements for harmony and gave loyalty to the serpent. They believed and put their faith in the serpent over God's authority. Disharmony is caused by rebelling from the ordained mandates of creation. Disharmony causes separation from God through a person's own choice. The spirit of a person is no longer in sync or in harmony with God's spirit. Darkness invaded the spirit body of Adam and Eve contaminating pure light. A domino effect within their soul bodies followed the original rebellion. Immediately, Adam sensed a closing of the spiritual connection to God. The Glory of God that had surrounded Adam was gone and he perceived himself naked. This led to fear of disapproval from God, as indicated by hiding from God (Genesis 3:10). Knowledge of evil taught him that punishment was a possibility for rebellion. This knowledge, along with fear, bred torment within the soul of Adam. Knowing what had happened in the garden, God entered the garden to offer his grace to Adam. God confronted Adam and gave him mercy. He did this when he asked him, "Where are you?" in Genesis 3:9. God did not focus on the disrespect or rebellion. God offered them a chance through confession and repentance when he asked, "Who told you were naked?" and, "Did you eat the fruit of the tree I told you not to eat?" in Genesis 2:11. A soul filled with fear is in tune with punishment as stated in 1 John 4:18:

> *There is no fear in love; but perfect love casts out fear because fear involves torment. But he who fears has not been made perfect in love.*

The desires that led to the rebellion allowed the perfect love for God to be clouded with the knowledge of separation from God. The possibility of committing acts that resulted in punishment sprang up in the souls of Adam and Eve. Fear, blame, shame, guilt and lying were choices made in the souls who now knew torment. This act closed the spiritual ears and eyes within the spiritual bodies of Adam and Eve. Without a fully functioning spirit body, a person no longer knows at the spirit level what is the will of God.

God's actions are consistent within Himself. God offered Adam the same opportunity He offers all who live on the other side of the cross of Jesus. Knowing the spiritual union with God and Adam had been broken by rebellion, God first sought out Adam. God was offering **grace**. God chose to delay judgment for the rebellion by giving

mercy to Adam. Next, God extended the opportunity for **forgiveness**. By allowing Adam to claim and **repent** of the rebellion, God extends a way to return to right relationship to Him. These four attributes of God are what Jesus Christ, the last Adam, renewed for all people. Jesus Christ willingly submitted to becoming sin, the product of rebellion, so His blood could be offered for atonement of our rebellion. As stated in 1 Peter 2:24:

> *...who Himself bore our sins in His own body on the tree, that we, having died to sins, might live for righteousness—by whose stripes you were healed.*

We receive this reunion with God through the same process that was offered Adam.

- ➢ God offers Grace in mercy.
- ➢ Admission of personal rebellion against God's authority in our lives and accepting Jesus' death for our own rebellion is accepting God's mercy.
- ➢ In exchanging our unrighteousness and earned harvest of death for the death of Jesus Christ in our place, we accept God's Grace.
- ➢ In receiving forgiveness from God, right relationship with God is restored.
- ➢ When one seeks God and His Kingdom to rule in our lives, this is the action of repentance.

The choice is ours to move back into proper relationship with God and His Kingdom or to remain in rebellion.

Think and Write about it

1. What is God's Kingdom pattern to return to right relationship with Him?

2. How does fear cripple the opportunities given for reconciliation to God?

2

Rooted and Built Up In Christ

Jesus Christ is the first born of the new creation of humanity. Those of us who have accepted Him as Lord and Savior are to grow in His likeness. As stated in Colossians 2:6 – 7 (NIV):

So then just as you have received Christ Jesus the Lord, continue to live in him,
⁷rooted and built up in him and strengthened in the faith as you were taught,
and overflowing with thankfulness.

To live in Christ is to surrender one's old reference points within the soul-heart. To be one in mind and heart with Jesus is to live in Him. It is the tearing away of the old to make room for the new reference points in the soul-heart. Jesus told his disciples that on a certain day they would know Jesus was in them. As recorded in John 14:20

"At that day you will know that I am in My Father, and you in Me, and I in you."

The acceptance of this reality is an act of faith. The action is the process of allowing the Holy Spirit to speak to the awakened and renewed spirit body of a person. This action is also a surrender of the old ways. A suspension of previous soul-mind reality is necessary for a person to hear spirit-to-spirit. It creates a space in the soul-mind without judgment. By being baptized in the Holy Spirit, a pathway is set within the soul-mind to hear the spirit-mind. The action of speaking in tongues is verifying within a person this pathway is open. It is a conscious pulling down of one's re-born spirit-mind to communicate with the soul-mind. Some believers describe the baptism of the Holy Spirit as the letting go of previous understanding and trusting the Holy Spirit to fill them with a greater presence. A living, active relationship with the Holy Spirit is the outcome of the baptism of the Holy Spirit. To live in Jesus is to communicate Spirit-to-spirit through faith.

Think and Write about It

Do you remember when you knew for sure that you lived in Jesus Christ as well as Jesus Christ living in you? What is your evidence you know this now?

Rooted in Christ Jesus

The method of being built up in Jesus Christ is applying spiritual tools to form spiritual habits. These habits strengthen a relationship with God. The basic spiritual tools are:

- ➢ Praise
- ➢ Meditating on the Bible
- ➢ Time spent in prayer closets
- ➢ Searching for God in daily life
- ➢ Daily surrendering one's will to God
- ➢ Giving God thanks

We can jump into practicing these tools before surrendering our will to our God. This creates muddy waters in understanding the ways of God. Instead of jumping into doing a method, God calls His people into personal relationship first. Faith and surrender are the avenues to this relationship. The new believer knows what not to do yet does not know how to form a personal relationship with God. The old reference points within the soul-heart create a temptation to do something that is pleasing to God before being vulnerable to God. Being built up in Jesus Christ begins with a relationship with God.

A reborn person in Christ Jesus is committed to seeking a personal relationship with God. There is danger in seeking actions before surrendering to God. This is why Jesus said, "...seek first the Kingdom of God..." (Matthew 6:33). Our eyes are to search for the spiritual truth of our Savior! This is accomplished in the spiritual realm. Faith is the vehicle used to access the spiritual realm. We need to build spiritual organs in our spirit bodies to take off the blinders and walk in the light of Jesus Christ. If we attempt the method before growing these spiritual organs, we are simply doing spiritual activities from the soul body perspective. When repenting of old ways of life, that includes forms of knowing and doing. It is letting go of one's own understanding (Proverbs 3:5). It is a daily surrender, asking the Holy Spirit to direct one's pathway. If we move directly into method, we still have the same earth centered compass to measure success or failure that we used before accepting Jesus as Lord. This approach, using my understanding and will is not walking in faith. For faith is evidence of what is not seen with physical eyes (Hebrews 11:1). To the new believer it is uncomfortable. Walking in the spirit seems like walking down a dimly lit alley with a blindfold on, trying to sense where to go. Faith is trusting that our unseen knowing God is leading. This is why knowing in the spirit is so important. It is believing wherever God leads is better than what one did before one surrendered to God as Lord. This faith is trusting the nature of God above self-preservation. Faith is trusting in all Jesus is and has accomplished as being the best way to go forward without seeing the pathway where one is walking. As stated in 2 Corinthians 5:7:

For we walk by faith, not by sight.

Using the first method, praise, will demonstrate the difference between soul knowing and spiritual knowing. Gratitude for escaping the old way of living and thinking guides praising God. A freshness enters the heart of the believer to give thanks for the freedom now known in the new life. Praise songs that seem to reflect the heart condition of the believer are sought. As time passes, the newness and joy of being a new creation in Jesus wears off. If the soul-heart with the old habits of thinking have not been cleansed, then praise simply takes the place of whatever music one preferred in the old lifestyle. It is not seen as something to give to God, but rather something to listen to as an encouragement to the believer. This causes believers to fit praise into a niche in their lives rather than raising up a new activity in daily life. Praise becomes a convenience, rather than a form of honoring God.

On the other hand, if a person is seeking the Kingdom of God and a relationship with Jesus Christ, daily surrender of one's will happens. Praise is a love song to my God who saves and provides for all my needs. God is the beloved one. I am asking God for directions about what to do and how to handle situations as I place myself under His authority through praise activities. I am not trusting myself to find solutions on my own. In this approach, I find new gratitudes. Each day as I follow God's directions rather than mine, I have new things to thank God for accomplishing. Ownership of my actions dies as gratitude for what God does through me rises. It leads to praising and honoring God. I see the results of trusting God as evidence of faith manifested in my life. Since I am learning how to apply faith, I am more aware of what is going on around me. I am giving mercy to fellow workers with whom I did not have patience before knowing Jesus as Lord. I surrendered the problems of work and frustration to God. It was a struggle to do this, yet I trusted God's word and applied my faith. Instead of focusing on the frustration and reviewing events, I began praising God in my mind or out loud. I find I am more at peace with the outcomes than when I tried to "put up with" the workers before on my terms. Now I have something fresh and new to praise God for accomplishing. My spiritual eyes are opening through my trust as I apply faith to the situations. Entering praise in church services has more meaning because I am truly thankful for the peace I now know at work. I want to thank God for what he has done for me. I even thank God when things are happening, rather than simply waiting to praise Him in church. Proverbs 3:6 - 7 comes alive in my soul-heart.

6In all your ways acknowledge Him, And He shall direct your paths. 7Do not be wise in your own eyes; Fear the LORD and depart from evil.

My faith is alive within me, and I start to seek opportunities to surrender to God and give Him praise. Trust in God has increased, and I am being built up in my spirit through resting in Jesus Christ.

God is seeking a personal relationship with his children. Just like in any relationship, this requires getting to know the other person. Seeking God is time consuming. As in any building of a trusting relationship with another person, it requires suspending judgment as we seek to understand the other person's point of view. So, surrendering one's will daily to God is the active suspension of judging God. It is listening to his point of view and seeking God's wisdom in all I do in life. This is the essence of how to approach God. Surrendering is also honoring God for all He is. Embracing Jesus Christ as the living embodiment of God is again a surrendering to God. As Jesus stated in John 14:23 - 24

> *[23]Jesus answered and said to him, "If anyone loves Me, he will keep My word; and My Father will love him, and We will come to him and make Our home with him. [24]"He who does not love Me does not keep My words; and the word which you hear is not Mine but the Father's who sent Me.*

The pathway to God is through knowing and loving Jesus Christ as Lord. Loving Jesus is honoring Him and placing Him above selfish desires. Keeping His words is the outcome of love. It is the evidence of respect and love. The doing follows the seeking of a love relationship, not the other way around.

It is true to know God we are to seek Him in his Word. The same approach with meditating on the Word of God through faith is applied to the doing activity of reading the Bible. Scripture is to be eaten or chewed upon. This is not simply memorizing words. Below is a short list of some of many ways to chew on the words:

- ➤ Applying the words of scripture to one's life is chewing on them.
- ➤ Compare it to other places in Scripture where God speaks of similar things. Such phrases as "fire of God" or "righteousness" deserve in-depth comparisons.
- ➤ Study the main words in Hebrew and Greek to pull out deeper cultural meanings
- ➤ Make the words personal and claim them as true for you.
- ➤ Study the lives of the people in the Bible to find their humanity and how faith transformed them. Seek how these traits may be in you.
- ➤ Study just the words of Jesus to find the characteristics of God. Write them out.

God's words to Joshua as he began his new role as leader of the Israelites can be applied to chewing on the words as well as an example of how to do this in faith. New believers are moving into unknown spiritual territories. Their guide is the voice of God as given to them by the Holy Spirit. Promises have been given by God for being in the likeness of Jesus and possessing his righteousness. The instructions to Joshua can be applied to these new believers regarding how to walk in faith.

Joshua had been mentored under Moses during the forty years in the desert. He was anointed and appointed by God through Moses to lead after Moses' death. At the beginning of the book of Joshua, these instructions are given to Joshua. Joshua 1:6 – 9

> *⁶"Be strong and of good courage, for to this people you shall divide as an inheritance the land which I swore to their fathers to give them. ⁷Only be strong and very courageous, that you may observe to do according to all the law which Moses My servant commanded you; do not turn from it to the right hand or to the left, that you may prosper wherever you go. ⁸This Book of the Law shall not depart from your mouth, but you shall meditate in it day and night, that you may observe to do according to all that is written in it. For then you will make your way prosperous, and then you will have good success. ⁹Have I not commanded you? Be strong and of good courage; do not be afraid, nor be dismayed, for the LORD your God is with you wherever you go."*

Here is a summary of the advice from God to Joshua about how to proceed in faith, trusting God to lead and provide for him:

- ➤ Stand in courage, do not be afraid for I, your God, go with you.
- ➤ Your strength is in my promised spoken word for you to succeed.
- ➤ Follow me, not your own understanding, and you shall prosper.
- ➤ Obey my instructions as I gave them to Moses as Kingdom principles.
- ➤ Meditate on my book of Kingdom laws day and night.
- ➤ Do not sway to the left or the right in understanding my principles.
- ➤ Know that I go with you wherever I lead you.

These words form a personal pattern of how to walk in faith and trust God. Living on the other side of the cross of Jesus, our covenant is in the blood of Jesus. All of God's words in His Bible teach us Kingdom of God principles to follow and stay on the straight pathways of God. By owning these instructions and practicing these words, a person walks in faith. This means to personalize them. Daily owning of the words helps to write them on the soul-heart of a believer. Pausing before acting and checking to see if I am following these principles makes them personal to me. The process is acknowledging God's words are true. Declarations such as those write

God's words deeper on our soul-hearts. Believing the promises of God will be achieved as I live within the bounds of them is a faith walk. I am moving by what is not seen, but what is hoped for when I surrender my actions to the guidelines in these words.

Think and Write about it

1. Why is it important to surrender one's will to God daily?

2. Give an example of a time you applied faith to a situation. How did God solve it? Did you give Him praise for it?

Battling the Old Soul-Heart

As noted in earlier chapters, there is a battle within the soul body between the pull of the old way of living and thinking and surrendering to Christ Jesus as Lord. There are two parts to this battle. The first is the crucifixion of the old soul's strongholds within the soul body. The second is the daily surrendering to writing new truths on the soul body. These are not achieved at the same time. Each is accomplished separately. When believers try to mix these two actions at the same time, they have open warfare on two fronts. No one can overcome this way! Jesus promised his disciples aid in bringing His presence into their spirits (John 14:16 – 18). The aid is the Holy Spirit. He will direct a person through this process of destroying the old soul-heart. What was created in the old life and written on the soul-heart must die before the new can take hold. If it not destroyed, it would contaminate the new wisdom being written on the soul-heart. One form of a double-minded condition in a soul-mind is created when the old reference points are not eradicated. It is like planting a garden without removing the weeds first. Both will grow together. Usually, the weeds will choke out the cultivated seeds.

The old soul-heart is to be crucified. Galatians 2:20 declares the completion of the spiritual truth of being crucified with Christ. Spiritual realities are to be completed in spiritual realms by spiritual actions. The spiritual actions are confessing, repenting, and applying the blood of Jesus to the structures built within the soul body of the believer. God created us in Their likeness. We share spiritual attributes with Them. One is we can create. Creation is not grounded in the transitory earthly realm. It is spiritual in nature. Remember, the soul is spiritual. What grows and is planted in the soul is done with spiritual energy. Creative acts are not limited to physical projects. We also create in our minds. Soul and spirit are both eternal and spiritual entities. It is in the spiritual realm creative acts happen within the soul-mind.

Building Unintended Structures

As we learn to exist in our families and our environments we write memories on our soul-minds. Some of the these are good memories and others are not. Within our soul-hearts we develop a standard of what brings the good and what brings the not so good. Unfortunately, this is done at an early age when our ability to fully understand events is limited. A child of two may learn that crying loudly either brings what is desired or some other child will learn it brings anger and punishment. The child does not understand it is also the demeanor of the adult who responds which is included in the results of the child's actions. The three and then four-year-old will now apply this warped pattern of success or failure to get what the child wants. We witness this in stores when children act out their wants with their adults. These memories also write beliefs about how life works on the soul-heart of the child. Children learn to appease adults, manipulate them, obey them, avoid them, or ignore them to achieve the children's desires. As a child grows and experiences life, other sources feed the soul-heart. What is seen on TV, video games, and heard in music fills in the gap of explaining interactions for good things and not so good things to enter the life of the person. Opinions and explanations by other adults or older children are grafted into the child's soul-heart. Attitudes such as the child is smart, or attractive, or athletic, or valued are added to the soul-heart. Sometimes the opposite is added such as the child is dumb, destructive, useless and a burden are written on the soul-heart. Decisions about who to trust and who to manipulate are also written on the soul-heart based on how love is satisfied. Some children learn to defend themselves against attacks of others and some learn to appease the attackers. All of these experiences build structures in the soul-heart to support a belief system about how to survive in the earthly realm.

These structures are spiritually built strongholds to defend and protect what the child believes. They are spiritual substances within the soul body. Trust, love, and faith can build these centers. They form healthy boundaries that allow a person to flow in relationships with those found trustworthy. A barometer or trust meter is a structure created in the soul-heart. Also fear, a spiritual opposite of faith, builds structures. Events that destroy trust build structures of doubt. When encouraged by others, doubt may build self-blame and guilt as walls within these structures. These can surround the soul-heart and form hardened structures based on fear of reoccurrences of similar experiences. Since the experiences of people are based on incomplete wisdom (lacking the input form the spiritual body) both types of structures are built in people. Even a redeemed young person, growing in Christ, may have inadvertently built some structures out of fear. Opening one's soul eyes and ears to material that honors the devil and builds fear can start the building of these structures in a child who is saved. Attacks against the character of a young person that are full of half-truths can also build negative structures.

This compass within the soul-heart is now used to judge with the soul-mind. Most people do not examine these structures after they have been built. Instead, people look at the actions driven by the soul-heart. Some will look at coping mechanisms of the person such as pride, bullying, people pleasing, competitiveness, or seeking compromises with half-truths, to name a few. All of these structures that are not in alignment with the Kingdom of God are to be crucified with Christ. Jesus Christ gave His believers a way to accomplish this task.

Think and Write it out

1. Describe some events in your childhood helped form your opinion of yourself.

2. What false ideas of your abilities did you overcome as an adult?

3. Who was most influential in forming your character?

Crucifying the Old Soul-Heart

Believers are to be one with Jesus Christ. Galatians 2:20 calls for identifying with the action of crucifixion.

> *I have been crucified with Christ; it is no longer I who live, but Christ lives in me; and the life which I now live in the flesh I live by faith in the Son of God, who loved me and gave Himself for me.*

It is seeing one's transgressions and rebellious manners being overlayed onto the slow death of Jesus Christ. Jesus stood in the gap, became our sin, and took our death. In the spiritual realm we are to experience this and surrender all these rebellious structures built in our soul-heart to die with him.

Jesus instituted the communion commonly called the last supper with his disciples before going to the garden of Gethsemane. It is by the blood of Jesus we are redeemed. Hebrews 9: 13 - 14

> *13For if the blood of bulls and goats and the ashes of a heifer, sprinkling the unclean, sanctifies for the purifying of the flesh, 14how much more shall the blood of Christ, who through the eternal Spirit offered Himself without spot to God, cleanse your conscience from dead works to serve the living God?*

Jesus told his disciples to take his blood and body and eat it for the forgiveness of sins (Mathew 26: 27 – 29). Jesus is describing a spiritual act within the spiritual realm. A believer is to take each rebellious act, thought, and attitude to the cross and surrender it to the blood of Jesus. In addition, every stronghold built in the soul is to be crucified. As mentioned earlier, the pattern is confession, repentance, and applying the blood. Each drop of Jesus Christ's blood carries reconciliation for various actions, thoughts, and attitudes. Returning to right relationship with God is an act of submission. In this spiritual act, the old understanding is held up to the truth of God. The Holy Spirit will convict the believer of what is false and outside the will of God. As stated in John 16:8

> *And when He has come, He will convict the world of sin, and of righteousness, and of judgment.*

Start the process with the first drops of blood Jesus shed. In addition to stating these words, taking communion with this process seals the statements. It is entering into the covenant of the blood of Jesus at a deeper level. In the Garden of Gethsemane Jesus shed blood from his forehead in his sweat (Luke 22:44). Here Jesus surrendered his will to God. The following steps are a process for breaking the strongholds of self-direction within the soul-heart. As with anything that a believer does with God, speaking out loud is committing one's heart and will to the statements. Feel free to use your own words to state these ideas, but speak with a sincere heart, for God does know a person's heart. This is a spiritual act completed in the spiritual realm through the redeemed spirit of the believer.

> ➤ **Confess:** I have chosen a lifestyle that satisfies me. My soul-heart has driven me to first find what will promote what I want or need before seeking Your will. I used my past experiences to avoid what is hurtful to me and obtain what works best for me. I have not always sought Your will God in all my actions. I have justified myself by claiming I am a good person. I have

compared my actions to others to justify my righteousness. I have not always sought Your ways. I have leaned into my own understanding over Yours.

➤ **Repent**: Forgive me, God, for not seeking Your will first. Forgive me for my impatience when I sought my way rather than waiting for You to build the pathway. Forgive me for not acting in trust that you would provide for me. Forgive me for not relying on Your love for me and seeking my own solutions. For I have sinned against You alone and done what is not righteous in Your sight (Psalm 51).

➤ **Apply the Blood**: I recognize the blood from the brow of Jesus was shed for choosing my way over Your way, God. I surrender my will to You God. I cover my actions with the blood of Jesus. As my savior demonstrated, I now say," Thy will be done, not mine." As stated in Psalm 103:12, You, God, have removed my transgressions as far as the east is from the west.

➤ **Take communion**: State, "By this bread I break any ungodly structures I have built in my soul-heart and soul-mind. I specifically break the structures I created out of self will to satisfy my desires. In the broken body of Jesus Christ, I have wholeness." Eat the bread. Lift up the cup symbolizing Jesus' blood. By this blood I cleanse any past actions, thoughts, and attitudes that placed my authority and will above God's will. I no longer stand on my righteous acts. It is the righteousness of Jesus Christ on which I now stand. By this blood I give all authority for my life to Jesus Christ.

➤ **Accept the Grace of God**. Jesus Christ's blood is the final cleansing agent. Do not give the enemy a foothold and question whether you are cleansed. Do not think this has to be done repeatedly. This past of choosing self-will over God's will is now dead. If any temptation or thought arises to claim anything else, simply state it is already covered in the blood of Jesus. As Jesus himself stated, "it is finished." If, at a later date, the Holy Spirit convicts you of acting in self-will over God's will, simply immediately repent and ask God to forgive you. Stand in faith, claiming the blood of Jesus has given you the righteousness of Christ. Then give praise to God for His victory through Jesus Christ.

The pattern is now applied to all places Jesus shed his blood. The Holy Spirit will convict believers of strongholds in their soul-hearts that they need to take to the cross for crucifixion. It is in seeking an intimate relationship with God that conviction happens. A believer is to spend time daily in mediating on scripture, praying, and praising God. Habits are to be formed in seeking God. In these times, the Holy Spirit will draw attention to structures still in the soul-heart that conflict with the Kingdom of God principles. At those times, take them to the cross, following the patterns listed above.

Here is a further example of applying the blood of Jesus. Jesus was beaten by those from the high priest while in their custody (Luke 22:63). These acts of violence were blatant disrespect for the authority and kingship of Jesus Christ, the Son of God. The guards were placing their loyalty to the authority of the ruling priesthood above loyalty to God. The guards allowed man's interpretation of the laws of God to rest in the hands of men. An example of this type of rebellion is when a person questions God's requirement for tithing. There are other things that this blood from the beating by the guards is needed to cleanse. This is just one example of playing word games while interpreting scripture to justify not obeying God's Kingdom Principles. The person is stepping outside of the written word of God and trusting the interpretation based on human understanding. When the same person seeks others to agree with their justifications, the person is placing agreement with man's wisdom above God's. For the believer in Christ as Lord, the Holy Spirit is the one who is to help interpret scripture (John 14:26). The following is applying the pattern of confession through reconciliation listed above to the sin of denying the authority of God in one's finances.

> ➤ **Confess**: I have sought man's ways of interpreting Your word God rather than seeking answers in Your word with the aid of the Holy Spirit. I have sought others to agree with my interpretations to justify my desire not to give more to the church. I have used my lack of agreement with how the church uses funds to withhold what you require of me, God. I have refused to tithe to You, God. I have not followed Malachi 3:10. I have broken covenant with You, God, by rebelling against Your written word for my own gain.

> ➤ **Repent**: Forgive me for my self-focus. Forgive me for not trusting You with my finances. I have raised my finances up to be a demi-god, worshipping its power to provide for me. Forgive me for being like the guards who beat Jesus by being loyal to man's wisdom to interpret Your words, God. I surrender my finances to You, God. I commit to tithing as Your word describes it. For I have sinned against You alone and done what is not righteous in Your sight (Psalm 51).

> ➤ **Apply the Blood**: I take the blood that came from the face of Jesus as He was beaten by the guards to cover my rebellion against Your authority in my life, God. I cover myself with this blood to wash away my selfishness and lack of trust in You. This blood from the face of Jesus is breaking the selfish structures I built in my soul-heart around money and tithing.

> ➤ **Take Communion**: I take this broken bread to cover the covenant I broke when I chose to seek opinions and sources outside of Your word and directions of the Holy Spirit. In your brokenness, Jesus, I am made whole. I take the blood from the face of Jesus to cover my rebellion in choosing man's rules and government over your Kingdom, God. As stated in Isaiah

53:5, you were pierced for my transgressions, Jesus, and this blood brings peace between me and God. Thank you for reconciling me to Father God.

> ➤ **Accept the Grace of God**. Praise God for restoring covenant with Him. Praise Him for being the sacrifice for your self-focus. Accept the new relationship and procced by asking God to show you how to handle your finances and giving.

As stated earlier, each drop of blood cleanses different acts, thoughts, and attitudes buried in the soul-heart before a person confessed Jesus Christ as Lord. Studying the crucifixion in detail and writing the truth of God's Words through the spirit body will reveal how each blood droplet cleanses the soul. As stated in 1 John 2:27 – 28

> *[27]But the anointing which you have received from Him abides in you, and you do not need that anyone teach you; but as the same anointing teaches you concerning all things, and is true, and is not a lie, and just as it has taught you, you will abide in Him.*

This anointing is received through the baptism of the Holy Spirit. A believer is sealed in the Holy Spirit. There is a direct connection between the believer's spirit and the Holy Spirit. Now that surrender and seeking a personal relationship are foremost in the intentions and habits of the believer. The methods come alive through the spirit body. By daily seeking God in one's prayer closet, praise and mediation on scripture, a closer intimate relationship is developed with God. A person learns to hear the Holy Spirit. Paul summarizes this relationship as recorded in 1 Corinthians 2:12 – 13

> *[12]Now we have received, not the spirit of the world, but the Spirit who is from God, that we might know the things that have been freely given to us by God. [13]These things we also speak, not in words which man's wisdom teaches but which the Holy Spirit teaches, comparing spiritual things with spiritual.*

Think and Write about it

Consider the blood that dripped down Jesus Christ's hands every time He held on to get another breath. What personal actions have you completed with your own hands that may dishonor God? What good actions have you committed of which you take ownership and have not given the glory to God? Use the process listed above and take it to the cross.

Writing God's Truth on One's Soul-Heart

The second battle is to write new guidelines onto the cleansed soul-heart. Those believers who have crucified themselves with Christ Jesus are now aware that Jesus

Christ lives in them. They have accessed the spiritual realm through their faith. They have practiced surrendering to God's will over their own desires and ideas. An intimate relationship with Jesus Christ is built daily. Holy Spirit has led them into developing their spiritual ears, eyes, and eyes of understanding to function in the spiritual realm. The daily surrender of self in relationship with God is a way of life. The habits of meditating on scripture, praising God, declaring God's truths, and submitting one's will in prayer are the spiritual acts completed in the spiritual realm that win the second battle in the soul body. Paul summarized this concept in Romans 12:1 – 2

> *I beseech you therefore, brethren, by the mercies of God, that you present your bodies a living sacrifice, holy, acceptable to God, which is your reasonable service. ²And do not be conformed to this world, but be transformed by the renewing of your mind, that you may prove what is that good and acceptable and perfect will of God.*

All three bodies are to be an integrated, living sacrifice to God. We are the living temple of God through Jesus Christ. In a sanctified believer of Jesus Christ, God lives in these three bodies as noted in John 14:23.

> *Jesus answered and said to him, "If anyone loves Me, he will keep My word; and My Father will love him, and We will come to him and make Our home with him.*

To love another is to choose to join in unity with them. Loving God is the driving force behind seeking God's will. Acting in unity with God's will is aligning with the Kingdom of Heaven principles. As stated in John 15:10

> *"If you keep My commandments, you will abide in My love, just as I have kept My Father's commandments and abide in His love.*

Loving, obeying, and surrendering are acts of abiding in God. Living a life in agreement with the Kingdom of God principles is serving God's purpose and original intent for humanity. It is acceptable service. Yet the service begins with surrender of one's will to the will of God. The old soul-heart has died. The renewed soul-mind becomes dependent on the Biblical words written of the soul-heart. What is good and acceptable in God's Heavenly Kingdom is to be written on the soul-heart. As stated in Philippians 4:8

> *Finally, brethren, whatever things are true, whatever things are noble, whatever things are just, whatever things are pure, whatever things are lovely, whatever things are of good report, if there is any virtue and if there is anything praiseworthy— meditate on these things.*

God's words are given in alignment with the will of God and the heavenly Kingdom principles. These words that a person meditates on, become the new compass for deciding actions within the soul-mind.

Think and Write about it

How are *loving God* and *seeking His will* related?

How does one make their three bodies into a holy living sacrifice? We align with the will of God. This alignment starts in the soul body. The daily surrender of personal will to the will of God focuses one's soul on the spiritual center above the earthly viewpoint. Just as God spoke life into darkness and created our world, so we his children are to speak into each day our agreement with His will. What we declare with our mouths reflects what is in our hearts or beliefs. As each day is new so is our verbal commitment to God aligning with the Kingdom of God. As stated in Proverbs 18:21

> *Life and death are in the power of the tongue. And those who love it will eat its fruit.*

Speaking our surrender to God's will is choosing life under the covenant of the Blood of Jesus. God's word states each day is a new day created by God (Psalm 118:24). As we enter into each new day, we are to claim who is our Lord. Through mediating on the Bible passages, we know who our God is. As in any love relationship, recognizing and honoring who the beloved is strengthens the relationship. Declaring who God is to us each day strengthens our relationship with God.

Declaring a surrendered will, praising God, and honoring Him for who He is becomes a reasonable service to begin a new day. Again, this is done through speaking or singing these declarations. Honoring God in praise for His attributes writes spiritual truths on the soul-heart. Reminding the soul-heart of these spiritual truths before being confronted with daily tasks reinforces our commitment and trust in God. Simple statements like those suggested below ground our souls in the spiritual truths.

- ➤ God's mercy is new every day
- ➤ God is faithful to all He promises
- ➤ God does not lie
- ➤ God is creator and greater than all He has created.
- ➤ God's wisdom is greater than any man's understanding

Again, find those truths which the Holy Spirit has led you to through mediation. The soul-will and soul-heart are now aligned with the will of God.

The rest of the verse of Romans 12: 2 describes how to algin the soul-mind to the new day. The *renewing of the mind* is the reasonable living sacrifice to complete the alignment of the soul body to the will of God. Thoughts bombard us when we awake from sleep. The soul-mind demands attention as it awakes to choices. Whether this awakening is from the need to plan or the voices of others placing demands for attention, it is still a pull from the worldly view to demand first place in the soul-mind. It can be simply an electronic input like music, TV, or a phone that pulls a person to focus on the world view over God's will. A habit of seeking God with one's soul-mind first thing after awakening will align the soul-mind with God's will. Time has become one of the most precious commodities of modern lifestyle. By placing a priority on entering one's prayer closet before being pulled into life's demands is also honoring God. For those who must respond to others before spending time in the prayer closet, declaring truths of God's words over oneself forces the soul-mind to prioritize the spirit. Some examples of scriptures about our identity as children of God are:

- ➢ I am God's child. (John 1:12)
- ➢ I have no fear, for God is on my side. (Psalm 118:6)
- ➢ I am a co-heir with King Jesus. (Romans 8:17)
- ➢ I have authority to trample on all the enemy brings against me. (Luke 10:17 – 19)
- ➢ I can do all things through Christ who strengthens me (Philippians 4:13)

As a believer meditates on the word of God, the Holy Spirit will lead you to find the ones to apply each morning to your soul-mind. These meditated words are to be written and spoken often. This practice writes them on the soul-heart. These thoughts become the new compass for the soul-mind to use to judge actions. As stated in 1 Peter 1:13 (NIV):

> *Therefore, prepare your minds for action; be self-controlled; set your hope fully in the grace to be given you when Jesus Christ is revealed.*

Our hope, the result of faith, is then focused on our source of grace, King Jesus. We are not easily enticed the ways of the world when we begin each day aligned in our souls with God's ways and will. In addition to declaring who we are in Christ Jesus, speaking in tongues accomplishes the same purpose of prioritizing spiritual connections within the soul-mind. All of these are ways of aligning the soul-mind of a person to the will of God.

Think and Write about it

1. Which scriptures have you meditated on that describe who you are in Jesus Christ?

2. What characteristics of God are most meaningful to you and give honor to God?

A significant set of tools for believers is the keys to the Kingdom of Heaven. Jesus asked His disciples who others said He was, and who they (the disciples) said He was. When Peter proclaimed Jesus to be the Messiah, Jesus stated an important truth about knowing how to use the keys of Heaven. Jesus stated Peter could only know this in his spirit. When Jesus said God the Father revealed it to Peter, He was recognizing the accomplishment of Spirit-to-spirit communications. Since this is only achieved through faith, it was Peter's faith that allowed his spirit body to hear the truth of who Jesus is. The process of accessing the keys of the Kingdom of Heaven is:

➢ Enter the spirit realm through faith

➢ Listen to the voice of God

➢ Speak what is given

➢ Give Honor to God for the revelation

These keys have been mainly used for intercession. They also serve the purpose of cleansing the soul-heart in declaring. It is not petitioning God, but rather coming in agreement with the principles of God's Kingdom.

In Matthew 16:19 Jesus stated:

> *And I will give you the keys of the kingdom of heaven, and whatever you bind on earth will be bound in heaven, and whatever you loose on earth will be loosed in heaven.*

To function at a deeper level in one's spirit body, a person cleanses one's soul-heart. The more the soul is cleansed, the easier it is to hear and know God's will. Listening and obeying God's will open greater revelation of Kingdom of Heaven principles. Our first place of authority as believers in Jesus Christ as Lord, is over our own bodies. After completing the steps of sanctification, it is each person's responsibility to keep the soul-heart clean. When one is aware of anger, anxiety, resentment or any other negative thought or emotion, it is our job to remove them. A simple act of stating, "In the name of Jesus I loose anger from my soul," cleanses the soul.

The next step is to bind the truth of God in the place of the destructive agent. Again, a simple declaration accomplishes this. For this declaration to live in the soul-heart, the person needs to be intimate with the spiritual truth of what is being declared. Intimacy is achieved when a person dwells on a particular spiritual truth. An example is Jesus stating that we may have peace (John 16:33).

"These things I have spoken to you, that in Me you may have peace. In the world you will have tribulation; but be of good cheer, I have overcome the world."

To become intimate with this spiritual truth, here are some steps to take. Ask yourself:

➢ How is this peace a comfort?

➢ How do I access it in my daily life?

➢ The Jewish people greet each other with Shalom or peace. Is this different from what Jesus said? How?

➢ Where else does Jesus talk about this peace?

➢ How is peace in Jesus different than the world's concept of peace?

➢ Where else does God describe this peace in His words?

Examine these passages and ask the Holy Spirit to lead you. Pray in tongues while reading the verses and ask for more understanding. Unfortunately for most of us, the negative things we write on our souls, such as anger and fear, we are well familiar with, yet the spiritual truths need to be studied to know them. The fruits of the spirit, the nature of God, and the words of His Son, Jesus Christ are some of the places for finding spiritual truths.

Declaring the words of the Bible and binding them to oneself allows them to grow in the soul body. Examples of such declarations are listed below.

➢ I bind the peace of God as only Jesus gives me to my soul body.

➢ I bind the joy of the Lord which is my strength to my soul body.

➢ I bind the mercy of God to my soul body to surround me as I drive today and loose this mercy on other drivers.

➢ I bind the grace of God to my soul body to overcome all my insufficiencies as I interact with co-workers today.

People do not need to wait for negative thoughts or emotions to rise in the soul body before binding God's truth to their soul bodies. It can be done first thing in the morning. Just like turning one's will over to God first thing in the morning, binding God's truth to one's soul-mind also creates a greater dependence on the spirit body.

Declaration is based on our authority as heirs through Jesus. Since Jesus lives in us, we possess His attributes. When we clean our soul-heart we remove the debris preventing us from rising higher into the spiritual realm. One of the abundant forms of debris in the soul-heart is unforgiveness. The soul-mind may have justified the unforgiveness by hanging onto the pain, rejection, or other types of hurt directed against a person. Others may believe they have forgiven someone but hang onto the memory of the events. Statements such as, "I forgive, but I do not forget," are examples of this. These actions deny unforgiveness and bury it deep in the soul-heart. Another may have been offended by the callous actions or words of another person. The offense is created when one person believes they are disrespected by another person. Many times, this happens within a mutually supportive relationship. The hard truth to swallow is that unforgiveness is self-focused or self-centered. It activates a person's will to take charge again of one's life over trusting God. Being pulled by unforgiveness in its many forms is activating the seeds of unbelief and doubt in God's ability to handle the situation. Looking downward into self prevents a person from keeping their eyes on God as Lord of all.

As stated in 1 Corinthians 6: 19 – 20

> *[19]Or do you not know that your body is the temple of the Holy Spirit who is in you, whom you have from God, and you are not your own? [20]For you were bought at a price; therefore glorify God in your body and in your spirit, which are God's.*

When we accepted Jesus Christ as Lord, we gave all authority to God over our lives. We promised not only to surrender to Him in that instance, but daily. We acknowledged His ways were better than ours. Through sanctification we have become His temple. Returning our focus to our own hurts and deciding they have greater importance than serving God, is rebelling against His authority. When these thoughts of refusing to forgive someone or only doing so with reservations arise, we are to turn to God. These challenges are to drive us into the strength of God and the blood of Jesus. These are situations in which to remember God's mercy and grace given to us in our time of need. If we believe God's grace is sufficient for us, we are to act upon this belief.

Paul states in Galatians 5:16

> *I say then: Walk in the Spirit, and you shall not fulfill the lust of the flesh.*

To walk in the spirit is to keep watch over one's soul-heart while keeping eyes on King Jesus. It is listening with spiritual ears to the conviction of the Holy Spirit. Returning to self-focus opens doorways to the world's views and man's wisdom over God's Kingdom of Heaven principles. Do we really trust God to provide for us? Do we trust God's words that in all things, He will never leave us or forsake us? Faith is hoping for what is not seen. It is trusting in the spiritual realm to come into our lives through our lord, King Jesus. Hebrews 11:1 is often quoted, but Hebrews 11:6 is necessary to continue to walk in faith. Hebrews 11:6:

> *But without faith it is impossible to please Him, for he who comes to God must believe that He is, and that He is a rewarder of those who diligently seek Him.*

Seeking is more than running to God on our own terms and at our convenience. We are to seek God in all our situations. The messier and more convoluted the situation is, the greater need we have to trust God. In times where pride is fed by hurt and rejection, seeking God may be difficult, yet needed. When we become a believer in Jesus Christ as Lord, the world has not changed. Our focus is to change and look to the spiritual, our place of origin and eternity. Our faith will be challenged by a world in rebellion to God's Kingdom principles. If God is our Lord we are to act on this faith, knowing beyond doubt God will honor our trust in Him.

We have come full circle now. We begin with faith and trust in what Jesus has accomplished. We surrender our will daily to our King Jesus. We write His truths on our soul bodies by accessing spiritual truth from God's words. We align our day through aligning all three of our bodies to the Kingdom of God principles. We feed our souls daily with the word of God, mediating on it. In all of this we keep our focus on our God, the provider and protector for His people. This is faith in action.

Think and Write about it

1. What spiritual truths do you need to daily bind to your soul body?

2. What new insights do you have about pride, self-focus and unforgiveness?

3

Fullness in Christ

Colossians 2:9 – 10

⁹For in Him [Jesus Christ] dwells all the fullness of the Godhead bodily; ¹⁰and you are complete in Him, who is the head of all principality and power.

Mature believers in Christ have awakened the fullness of Christ in themselves through spiritual work completed in the spiritual realm. Having written the word of God on their soul-hearts, their internal compass is in alignment with the will of God and the Kingdom of God principles. The soul body also has a soul-mind that has operated with the cloudy understanding from the worldview of life. Remember, the function of the soul-mind is to evaluate input from the physical world and spiritual world. When crucifying the old soul-heart, the soul-mind was placed in a nonjudgmental role. When reborn believers learn like children, the new soul-hearts are inscribed with the words of God in this objective manner. The re-birth of the soul-mind in Christ happens through a similar process as the soul-heart within the soul-mind.

Events in daily living bring choices. The soul-mind uses the soul-heart as a reference to interpret the events. The soul-mind can agree with the soul-heart and apply the principles to daily life events. It also has the ability to override the foundational wisdom of the soul-heart. Decisions about how to handle life are accomplished within the soul-mind. Attitudes, emotions, personal history, and beliefs of the soul-heart are applied through the soul-mind. It is here the senses of the world are intertwined with the compass of beliefs, attitudes, and emotions. In mature believers, the soul-mind has access to the spirit realm through the spirit body and the Holy Spirit. Spirit organs can be accessed through the soul-mind as it surrenders in an impartial approach. Just as writing God's words on the new soul-heart was done in an objective, yet spirit-filled attitude, now the soul-mind can apply wisdom pulled down through one's spirit in the decision-making process. As noted in earlier chapters, this is where the real battle with the enemy happens.

Think and write about it

1. What are two abilities of the soul-mind?

2. In mature believers, what is the advantage the soul-mind has?

God's enemy brings doubt and questions into the soul-mind. It began in the Garden of Eden when the serpent spoke to Eve in Genesis 3:1:

> *Now the serpent was more cunning than any beast of the field which the LORD God had made. And he said to the woman, "Has God indeed said, 'You shall not eat of every tree of the garden'?"*

God's command was written on the soul-heart of Eve. The condition for eternal life was obedience in surrendering one tree to God. The enemy's question focused on the provision, eliminating the condition. The enemy of our God uses this type of questioning to build doubt and mistrust of the words written on our soul-hearts. He plays word games with God's decrees and requirements to cause confusion and doubt. Even the temptations of Jesus were based on misinterpretations of God's recorded words in the Bible. A challenge based on doubt about who Jesus is was thrown at Jesus as recorded in Matthew 4:3:

> *Now when the tempter came to Him, he said, **"If** You are the Son of God, command that these stones become bread."*

Prove to me, man who you are by acting within your God-given rights. This temptation had many layers. One of the layers was to act without consultation with God whether functioning in this manner was currently within God's plans for Jesus. The enemy's statement implied Jesus had to prove to the world who He is. The challenge of operating within our own understanding is one all mature believers in Jesus Christ face. Mature believers are submitted to God. When activating the soul-mind, a mature believer is to use both what is available in the spirit body as well as what is known in the physical body. In fact, Jesus was hungry as indicated by his physical body. Checking his soul-heart, Jesus knows He is a three-body being whose spirit body also has needs. He may have accessed this spirit body also. Now the soul-mind searches for truth within the spirit wisdom written on his soul-heart. Jesus quotes Deuteronomy 8:3. He begins his answer with what is written on his soul-heart that is in alignment with the Kingdom of God principles. Jesus' choices break pride and reinforce dependency on God for life support.

The enemy, having failed to compromise Jesus, moves to the next level of temptation. If Jesus is going to quote scripture, then the enemy does, also. The enemy quotes a scripture of protection through the angels assigned to Jesus. Again, this temptation has many layers. For this discussion, the focus is on how Jesus applied the word of God within His soul-heart to defeat the temptation of misinterpretation of God's words. Jesus rises in his spirit body and finds a spiritual truth within the Kingdom of God principles. The overriding principle of dependency on God as creator, over what his creation, humankind, can accomplish is paramount in a life surrendered to God. Jesus' answer is recorded in Matthew 4:7:

> *Jesus said to him, "It is written again, 'You shall not tempt the LORD your God.'*

The soul-mind connects to the spirit body. In speaking spirit-to-spirit, Jesus owns two things. One, He is first a spiritual being created by God. Second, entering the spiritual body is an act of surrender to the authority of God in the realm of earth. One can only enter the spiritual body through submission and faith. Faith is based on the belief that God is alive and active in His creation. It is a trust in God who provides through faith for those who seek Him. In recognizing these two spiritual truths, Jesus' faith ignites the truths in His soul-mind. Jesus declares God's living word to overcome the twisting of God's words by the enemy. These two temptations are a small portion of what Jesus did in obedience to the authority of God. Jesus regularly applied Kingdom of God principles when deciding actions within his soul-mind.

Highlighted within the actions Jesus chose in these temptations is a hard-core spiritual truth within the Kingdom of God principles. It is the power of the word of God. Jesus' first statement, or verbal assault at the enemy, was, "it is written." As noted in earlier chapters, we are the likeness of God. Our words either speak life or death into our atmosphere. God's words are always full of life. When we stand in agreement with God's living words, we are bringing life into every situation. A Kingdom of God principle, when spoken with our mouths, creates in our earthly realm. In other words, what we believe in our hearts and speak with conviction plants seeds in the earthly realm. Paul describes this power of life of the word of God in Hebrews 4:12:

> *For the word of God is living and powerful, and sharper than any two-edged sword, piercing even to the division of soul and spirit, and of joints and marrow, and is a discerner of the thoughts and intents of the heart.*

The word of God recognizes the intents of a heart. A soul-heart that is devoted and surrendered to King Jesus is known by God. As noted earlier, the Holy Spirit is witness to this truth. When mature believers turn their soul-minds to their spiritual bodies and release God's words, a connection within the spiritual realm allows them to pull down into this realm the living power of God. Agreeing with them and declaring these words in faith activates them. Whatever the enemy has tried to place in the soul-mind is cut out and destroyed. As Paul stated, whether the attack is on the spiritual body, the soul body or the physical body, God's words can divide and cleanse what is not life from all three bodies, by applying eternal life through God's words.

Mature believers in Jesus Christ as Lord are filled with the fulness of Christ. We can apply our soul-minds in the same manner to life situations. It is a learned process we are called to practice daily. We are called to have the same mind as Christ. Paul states this, as recorded in Colossians 3:1 – 3

> *¹If then you were raised with Christ, seek those things which are above, where Christ is, sitting at the right hand of God. ²Set your mind on things above, not on things on the earth.*

This is what Jesus demonstrated in the two temptations described above. Setting our minds on things above is keeping the Kingdom of God principles not only in the soul-heart, but also in the actions of the soul-mind in union with the spirit body. We are to seek within our spirit bodies and consult them as often as we do our physical bodies when making choices. Paul concludes our soul-minds are not to concentrate on things of the earth, given to us from our physical senses. Simply decide what to do after submitting to fresh spiritual input. Standing in faith and declaring the words of God as absolute truths in our lives activates the sword of truth King Jesus redeemed for us by his death and resurrection. Doubt, fear, double-mindedness, and all negative emotions are overcome when our confidence is in the word of God as the absolute final authority. The enemy's tempting thoughts only enter our soul-minds as no more than a whisper to be brushed away with the truth of God's words. We are choosing life over death and chaos. We are demonstrating submission to our King Jesus above the works of the enemy in our world. We are turning our wills over to God and calling his Kingdom principles into our realm. This is what having the mind of Christ looks like. A Kingdom of God principle for those operating in the mind of Christ is to stand in faith, always declaring the word of God over every situation.

Think and write about it

1. How does God's enemy try to confuse the soul-mind of believers?

2. How does Jesus defeat the enemy?

Throughout the book of John, Jesus is quoted as stating this is how He decided what to do, knowing through his spirit body. One example of this is found in John 4:34:

> *Jesus said to them, "My food is to do the will of Him who sent Me, and to finish His work.*

The disciples returned from seeking food in a Samarian village. Jesus has just conversed with the woman at the well. When they tell him to feed his physical body, Jesus tells them he has food to eat. His choice to minister at the well to the woman was following the will of God. This action fed his spiritual/soul bodies. Jesus was led by spirit-to-spirit communication to speak as he did to the woman. The result was multiplication of salvations within the town in Samaria. We can relate these words to the temptation mentioned above about the stones. Amid the temptation and battling the enemy, Jesus fed his spirit by aligning with the will of God. Another Kingdom of God principle for those who operate in the mind of Christ is to always keep the soul-mind focused on the will of God.

Later, in the book of John, Jesus is called to defend his choice of healing on the Sabbath. Those attacking Him are religious leaders who are concerned about maintaining their own power. The people Jesus healed on the Sabbath were ones the other religious leaders were not able to heal. The opinion of the religious leaders was that this was a power grab by an unknown rabbi acting outside of their authority. His first statement to them, as recorded in John 5:17 reflects again, doing the will of Father God. John 5:17:

> *But Jesus answered them, "My Father has been working until now, and I have been working."*

Jesus chose the authority of God as his defense. As noted in the earlier quote, Jesus' will is surrendered to God to do the work of Father God. There is no division in the work between Father God and Jesus. The work is one and the same, the result of following the will of God. Jesus had the nerve to claim God as his Father. Scripture, in the creation story, also states humanity is God's offspring (Genesis 1:27). The religious leaders hung their authority on being children of Abraham above being God's offspring. They chose to limit God's authority to rules and regulations they interpreted from God's words. They proclaimed their authority from bloodlines under the covenant of sin and death given through Moses. Though Jesus followed and honored the Mosaic law, His authority was founded in His relationship as a son of man and son of God. Jesus' bloodline also included God through His holy conception. As Jesus submitted to God's will, Father God taught Him His Kingdom principles (Hebrews 5: 8 – 9, John 5:20). Jesus' work and His will gained authority as it flowed through heavenly realms into earthly realms. Jesus was telling them He aligned with the will and work of God for humanity. Committing to this agreement, Jesus had the authority to do what He was doing.

In the same encounter, Jesus further describes His obedience to God in John 5:19 -20:

> [19]*Then Jesus answered and said to them, "Most assuredly, I say to you, the Son can do nothing of Himself, but what He sees the Father do; for whatever He does, the Son also does in like manner.* [20]*"For the Father loves the Son and shows Him all things that He Himself does; and He will show Him greater works than these, that you may marvel.*

Through spirit-to-spirit communication, Father God shows Jesus what to do. Jesus was instructed in how to operate in Kingdom of God principles while in His fleshly body. Relating to God as a son, just like Adam did before his rebellion, Father God is teaching one who learns through obedience to God. It is recorded in Mathew 3:17 that a voice from heaven spoke when Jesus was baptized claiming Jesus as the Son of God. A love relationship between Jesus and Father God developed. Through this love relationship, as Jesus sought time with God, he was taught how to operate within Kingdom of God principles. The key is completely submitting in love to the will of God. Jesus pulled the wisdom gained in His spirit body into His soul-mind to learn and know Kingdom of God principles and how to use them while living in the physical body. A third principle for operating in the mind of Christ is listening to the voice of God in one's spirit body and obeying what God says to do. These patterns are accomplished in the soul-mind of the mature believer. This blending of complete submission to Father God as the foundation for Jesus' wisdom is further explained in the same chapter of John. As recorded in John 5:30:

> *I can of Myself do nothing. As I hear, I judge; and My judgment is righteous, because I do not seek My own will but the will of the Father who sent Me.*

A person can only operate with the fulness of the mind of Christ in one's soul-mind when there is no ownership of actions that proceed from directions from the spirit realm. Remember, the soul-mind evaluates. This is a form of judgment. The soul-mind decides how to proceed in life events. Surrendering to God's will and seeking it above any understanding filtered through the earthly worldview is suspending judgment. This is a spiritual act completed when one is in unity with one's spiritual body. The only way this judgment is righteous is when our own righteousness is crucified with Jesus on the cross. As stated in 2 Corinthians 5:21:

> *For He made Him who knew no sin to be sin for us, that we might become the righteousness of God in Him.*

We kill our own righteousness when we nail all our behaviors, attitudes, beliefs, and personal decisions to the cross. After that experience, it is our job not to slip back into building our own righteousness. Jesus operated in this complete union of His will always submitted to God's will. He reached into the spiritual realm through a cleansed soul-heart to grab God's righteousness as a guide for all He did. Thus, Jesus could truly say His judgment was righteous for it was in complete alignment with God's righteousness.

Think and write about it

1. How did feeding His spirit allow Jesus to fight the enemy?

2. What are three tools Jesus used to handle confrontation by the enemy?

Part of the assignment for a mature believer is to constantly cleanse and re-align all three bodies to the Kingdom of God principles. John explains in his letter, 1 John 3:3:

> *And everyone who has this hope in Him (Jesus Christ) purifies himself, just as He is pure.*

It is always accomplished through a daily act of surrender to God's will. A mature believer relies on the Holy Spirit to convict a person of anything that pulls away from this action (John 16:8). This cleansing is also a submission to the authority of the Holy Spirit in our lives. The truthful admission that without the direction of God, we can do nothing that pleases God is core to possessing the mind of Christ. As stated earlier, the battle with the enemy is for influence over the soul-mind (1 Peter 2:11). Our confidence is in Jesus Christ not our own thoughts, actions, or judgments. Our first reference is to our spiritual bodies, not the pull of earthly wisdom (Colossians 2:8). Our trust is in our God who redeemed us through Jesus Christ. Our faith rests in God's faithfulness. Staying under the covenant of the Blood of Jesus and the authority of God is honoring and living for God. This is walking in the spirit as recorded in Galatians 2:20. When these principles of how Jesus Christ listened and obeyed within his relationship with God are applied to Galatians 2:20, the mature believer can function with the soul-mind of Christ.

Think and Write about it:

1. Describe how the soul-mind overcomes the lies and half-truths of the enemy.

2. Write the three Kingdom of God principles Jesus applied when working for God.

The Great Deception

Jesus Christ in the flesh is a love offering from our God to His created people. One of the most quoted scriptures is John 3:16 -17.

> *16For God so loved the world that He gave His only begotten Son, that whoever believes in Him should not perish but have everlasting life. 17For God did not send His Son into the world to condemn the world, but that the world through Him might be saved.*

Through the obedience of Jesus Christ to the will of Father God, all things in heaven and earth are reconciled back to the divine order it was created to be (Colossians 1:19 – 22). Our holy and perfect God was separated from His creation, humanity, by the rebellion of Adam and Eve. Rebellion to divine order breeds chaos. Chaos destroys harmony and order. The seeds of rebellion and chaos are the actions known as sin. This destructive process creates death. Holy God separated Himself from the breeders and source of chaos, sealing off access to communion with heavenly realms to protect the heavenly realms (Genesis 3:23 -24). The reconciliation of all things through Jesus Christ is the second recorded time God cleansed His creation from corruption. The first time happened when Lucifer was removed from heaven for his rebellion against God (Isaiah 14:12 – 15). The courts of heaven decreed a specific requirement had to be met for humanity to return to its divine relationship with God. Only a representative of humanity who humbly submitted to God's requirements could re-open the access to heavenly realms while living in the earthly realm. It is a legal matter defined within the government of God's kingdom. Order and harmony with the laws of creation are required within the earthly realm for life to be abundant (Genesis 2:15 – 17 & Genesis 9:8 -10 & Deuteronomy 30:19). As recorded in Romans 5:17:

> *For if by the one man's offense death reigned through the one, much more those who receive abundance of grace and of the gift of righteousness will reign in life through the One, Jesus Christ.*

Life returns to humanity through being in harmony with Kingdom of God principles of government. Chaos is destroyed when order is returned through obedience and surrender to the authority of our living Holy God. Chaos and rebellion cannot exist when people truly embrace the covenant of the blood of Jesus. Without these chaotic, rebellious roots breeding in people, the actions of sins have no fertile ground within a soul body to grow. It is part of the covenantal promise of God to His people. As stated in John Chapter 3, Jesus becomes the avenue to obtain this life. Abundant life through Jesus grows in a person's soul body as they rise in faith and operate within their spirit body. What the enemy does not want the redeemed to know is that life is available in abundance now, while in our earthly bodies (John 10:10).

John further explains how this works in his first letter. As noted in 1 John 3:4:

Whoever commits sin also commits lawlessness, and sin is lawlessness.

Lawlessness is another name for chaos and rebellion. Lawlessness, or acting outside the divine order of creation is the root of the actions, sin. Unfortunately, through the spirit of religion, too many of church teachings focus on the action, sin, without dealing with the root, lawlessness. It is the willingness to deny the commitment to covenantal relationship with God that allows people to look to sin rather than the root. When sin is colored as an unfortunate slip caused by outside factors from our world cultures, the root of lawlessness is ignored. By continually focusing on the action of sin or resisting of sin, a person may slip into basing their relationship with God on their own righteousness. This puts people back into the law of sin and death, outside of the blood covenant with Jesus. It is a slippery slope, moving away from trusting and daily surrendering to God and into honoring self for not sinning. The roots of rebellion and chaos are eradicated from a soul body in daily submission to God. As long as a believer's foundation is in Jesus Christ as Lord, the soul body is good soil to grow God's words and birth the love of God in the believer.

When we accepted Jesus Christ as savior through grace, we surrendered to the authority of God in all of our life endeavors. Accepting the blood offering of Jesus Christ for our rebellion (our roots from previous lifestyles) is joining this covenant with God. Repenting is turning from the old references for life's understanding and accepting the Kingdom of God principles as governing our lives. John explains how sin, the action, is defeated in the relationship of covenant with God in 1 John 3:9:

Whoever has been born of God does not sin, for His seed remains in him; and he cannot sin, because he has been born of God.

Again, John is referring to the product of living in covenant with God under the grace of God through the blood of Jesus as destroying the roots of sin. Without the root of lawlessness living in our soul bodies, sin cannot grow in us. Instead, we have a seed of new life planted in us when we confess and accept Jesus as Lord.

Think and write about it

1. Explain the decree from the courts of heaven for bringing humanity back into divine relationship with God.

2. How does the *root* of sin differ from sin?

3. What is the danger when people focus on the sin and not the root of it?

Jesus Christ abides or lives in us. As John later states in 1 John 4:13

> *By this we know that we abide in Him, and He in us, because He has given us of His Spirit.*

During the time Jesus Christ instituted communion, He explained how this worked to His disciples. In John 15, Jesus describes the union of abiding in Him as the spiritual vine. In John 15:1 Jesus states:

> *I am the true vine, and My Father is the vinedresser.*

The life of God will be poured into believers through the living presence of Jesus Christ in the spirit/soul body of the believer. The relationship with Father God to the vine highlights the dependency of Jesus on the will and purposes of God. Father God shapes, feeds, and nourishes the vine to grow in the pattern Father God has chosen. Jesus lived through the will of God and completely submitted to God's directions when He walked the earth. They are one in purpose. Jesus tells his disciples in John 15:4 – 5:

> [4]*"Abide in Me, and I in you. As the branch cannot bear fruit of itself, unless it abides in the vine, neither can you, unless you abide in Me.* [5]*"I am the vine, you are the branches. He who abides in Me, and I in him, bears much fruit; for without Me you can do nothing.*

When we submit to the covenant of the blood and loving God as Jesus did, Jesus lives in our spirit/soul bodies through the seed planted by the covenantal agreement. This is the first part, Jesus abiding in us. We chose to abide or live for Jesus Christ as Lord. This second part, when we choose to abide in Jesus, is completed in the spiritual realm through applying the mind of Christ in our own soul bodies. Mature believers have cleansed their soul bodies to be good ground so this seed develops into a vine that can be formed by God.

Though the seed of faith is planted within us, and Christ dwells in us, it is our job to follow the Kingdom of God principles and grow this seed. John recognizes this truth when he states in 1 John 2:4 – 5:

> *⁴He who says, "I know Him," and does not keep His commandments, is a liar, and the truth is not in him. ⁵But whoever keeps His word, truly the love of God is perfected in him. By this we know that we are in Him.*

John rightly points to a soul-heart problem as not simply a failure to decide to obey. Believers are in a personal relationship with our God that supersedes the draw of the world. It requires a conscious, daily surrender and choosing God's Kingdom over what the world has to offer. John notes the application of God's words in union with God, creates in the believer the love of God in each believer. Instead of preventing the product of lawlessness, sin, John speaks of seeing God's love. Love is magnified within our souls, blocking any building of rebellious roots in our soul bodies. This is why John states in I John 4:7:

> *Beloved, let us love one another, for love is of God; and everyone who loves is born of God and knows God.*

The proof of a reborn soul and spirit body is the product of God's manifested love. Building an intimate relationship with God above all else breeds love for God. The core of Jesus' work rested on this intimate relationship. Knowing God at a deeper level is rising into one's spirit body and communicating spirit to spirit. Seeking and surrendering to God through Jesus Christ in covenant by His blood opens doors in the heavenly realms. In surrender, the true love of God for all He has created pours into the reborn person's three bodies. Now the love of God embraces the reborn person. In this unity a person returns love to God. As John states in 1 John 4:19:

> *We love Him because He first loved us.*

An intimate relationship with God is foundational to this type of obedience. God's solution was founded in love. Jesus' work is also rooted in love. Our obedience and surrender are established in love. Obedience and surrender of one's will bring a person only so far into relationship with God. Without love at the core, it is only loyalty. Loyalty is an action decided by the soul-mind. It can be influenced by the physical body and the traditions of the world. Decisions can be compromised. Returning love to the beloved is a product of gratitude. Seeking to live in the midst of the created love between two beings is abiding in love. It is developed through abiding in Christ. John 15:9 - 10 states:

> *⁹As the Father loved Me, I also have loved you; abide in My love. ¹⁰If you keep My commandments, you will abide in My love, just as I have kept My Father's commandments and abide in His love.*

Father God loves His only begotten son, Jesus Christ, with an all-encompassing, protective love. Whatever a good and righteous parent provides through love and care for a child is just a small shadow of what Father God's love is. Father God's love supports, provides, protects, nurtures, and pours blessings and strength into those who have submitted to His care and Kingdom of God principles just like He did for His son, Jesus Christ. As John stated in 1 John 4:16:

> *And we have known and believed the love that God has for us. God is love, and he who abides in love abides in God, and God in him.*

Since Jesus Christ is the door into reunion to Father God, we are called to abide in Jesus Christ's love. This love is the same love that took our transgressions and rebellions onto His person and went to hell, so we do not have to go there. This love is the same love that gave all power and authority Jesus achieved by destroying the enemy and his kingdom to His believers. Jesus' love for us is so much greater than we can comprehend. Jesus' love will encompass each person and give a place to abide and live in Jesus Christ and through Jesus Christ (1 John 4:10). This love has the power to destroy all chaos and rebellion. God's love is so powerful that He will not force truth on us but send grace to call us back to His love. Jesus Christ is the ultimate calling card of grace.

Think and write about it

1. Explain how Jesus abides in you.

2. How do we develop the seed of faith in our spirit and soul bodies?

Choices in Love

We are only asked if we want to join with this love and accept it by grace. We can choose to leave the chaos and rebellion against the Creator and enter into relationship with our God. We can blame God for the results of our rebellion and breaking covenant with Him. We can buy the lies of the enemy that the results of rebellion and chaos in our earthly realm are the fault of an all-powerful God. We can use these lies to beat up God. We can choose to lean on our own understanding, giving ourselves permission to meet all our desires in our own strength. God's magnificent love gives us the choice. In a relationship founded on love, not loyalty, freedom to accept or reject love is given. God's love created the Bible to explain Kingdom of God principles. God buried these Kingdom of God principles in His creation for all to see (Romans 1:20). Jesus went to hell to take back what was stolen by the enemy and end the bondage of death, hell, and the grave. Our risen King Jesus now controls those doors with those keys, not the enemy. Fear was broken when the keys were no longer in the hands of the enemy. As John explains, the power of fear is overcome by this love. 1 John 4:18:

> There is no fear in love; but perfect love casts out fear because fear involves torment. But he who fears has not been made perfect in love.

Those who choose to remain in rebellion and lawlessness still fear. For the only thing lawlessness has to offer is torment through subjugating others under the power of the enemy. The way out of lawlessness and its product, sin, is surrender to the love of God through the sacrifice of Jesus Christ. It is entering covenant by the blood of Jesus and accepting the magnificent, overpowering love of God for his creation. The enemy did not write the rules of life or determine the harmonies to keep everything functioning as intended by the Creator. God is our Creator. It is His design. Only through deception can the enemy convince someone he has control over creation. God's love is so much greater and overpowers all of the enemy's strategies. As stated in Romans 3:38 -39:

> [38]For I am persuaded that neither death nor life, nor angels nor principalities nor powers, nor things present nor things to come, [39]nor height nor depth, nor any other created thing, shall be able to separate us from the love of God which is in Christ Jesus our Lord.

God's love is pure with His intent that all He created shall be embraced and benefit from His love. The definition of divine love as recorded in 1 Corinthians 13: 5 – 7 includes:

> ...[5]does not behave rudely, does not seek its own, is not provoked, thinks no evil; [6]does not rejoice in iniquity, but rejoices in the truth; [7]bears all things, believes all things, hopes all things, endures all things.

God's love does not seek to impose His will on his created family, humanity. He asks us to enter covenant when He sends grace through Jesus Christ. God chooses to bear all our insults, rebellion, and accusations until we move into grace and surrender to His divine plan (2Peter 3:9). God provides opportunities through His people who claim Him as Lord to demonstrate God's divine love to others caught in lawlessness. His righteous structure of seedtime, growth time and harvest time is still functioning in every life within the earthly realm. God hopes those who choose to operate in rebellion and honor the lies of the enemy will wake up and return to Him. This is why Jesus taught the parable of the prodigal son (Luke 15:11 – 15). It is God who let the younger son take his inheritance and squander it in the world. It is God who loved him enough to let him go and hoped he would return. It is God who waited and watched, seeking evidence of his return. This is the love that bears all things, endures all things, and hopes all things. It is God who celebrates the return of the son and forgives all things done in rebellion to His divine order. Our unredeemed soul-minds trained by the world's standards cannot comprehend this type of love.

Immature soul-minds redeemed through accepting the gift of Jesus Christ as Lord are warned through the older son's story. Loyalty alone can breed resentment, pride, and judgmental attitudes for others. Only through an intimate love relationship with God do brothers and sisters in Christ know the truth of divine love. When we rest in God's love, He completes us. Our confidence is in this relationship. Knowing this divine love and truth in our spirit, we are called by our Father God to imitate Jesus Christ. 1 John 2: 6:

> *He who says he abides in Him ought himself also to walk just as He walked.*

God calls mature believers to trust the relationship with Him and to move out of self-interest, walking in the mind of Christ. As Paul describes in Philippians 2:1 – 3:

> *¹Therefore if there is any consolation in Christ, if any comfort of love, if any fellowship of the Spirit, if any affection and mercy, ²fulfill my joy by being like-minded, having the same love, being of one accord and of one mind. ³Let nothing be done through selfish ambition or conceit, but in lowliness of mind let each esteem others better than himself.*

Our confidence is in who God is and who we are as we abide in Jesus Christ. We are led by the Holy Spirit through spirit-to-spirit communication. We are to move into the world as ambassadors for the Kingdom of God with the same love, mercy, grace and forgiveness that God bestowed on us (2 Corinthians 5:20). We are to be the voice of God, just as Jesus was. We are to move in the divine love and offer to those caught in lawlessness the keys to enter the Kingdom of God. Our actions are to be filled with forgiveness, grace, mercy, and love. This is the hope of glory Jesus saw when He went to the cross (Colossians 1:27).

John states in 1 John 4:11-12:

> *[11]Beloved, if God so loved us, we also ought to love one another. [12]No one has seen God at any time. If we love one another, God abides in us, and His love has been perfected in us.*

Letting go of self-centered concerns is a step toward being in one accord with other believers. Our relationship with other believers begins with a common love and gratefulness for all God is. As stated in Colossians 3: 15 – 16:

> *[15]And let the peace of God rule in your hearts, to which also you were called in one body; and be thankful. [16]Let the word of Christ dwell in you richly in all wisdom, teaching and admonishing one another in psalms and hymns and spiritual songs, singing with grace in your hearts to the Lord.*

Peace through a soul-mind committed to becoming the mind of Christ is to rule us as we seek unity with other believers. When we know who we are as we abide in Jesus Christ, gratitude and praise overflows within us. We are to corporately express this love of God. It is our passion for God that invites Jesus Christ into our shared presence. God's love is multiplied in this expression of unity. These times are not simply for our own benefit. This practice of divine love is to feed God's people so they may now go into the world and complete the divine commission given by King Jesus (Mark 16:15 – 18 & Matthew 28:18 -20). God's divine plan of reconciling His creation back to its intended purpose includes the sons and daughters of God to claim their positions in His creation, this earth. Under the covenant of the blood of Jesus, believers are to demonstrate God's love to all people, no matter what their circumstances are. Once we learn how to abide in God and be in one accord with other believers through prayer and worship, we are to overcome the enemy with this divine love. This is the essence of Paul's prayer to the Ephesians recorded in Ephesians 3:16 -19

> *...[16]that He would grant you, according to the riches of His glory, to be strengthened with might through His Spirit in the inner man, [17]that Christ may dwell in your hearts through faith; that you, being rooted and grounded in love, [18]may be able to comprehend with all the saints what is the width and length and depth and height— [19]to know the love of Christ which passes knowledge; that you may be filled with all the fullness of God.*

Think and write about it

1. What does "abiding in God's love" look like to others?

4

Sons and Daughters of God

¹²But as many as received Him, to them He gave the right to become children of God, to those who believe in His name: ¹³who were born, not of blood, nor of the will of the flesh, nor of the will of man, but of God. John 1:12 - 13

Those who receive Jesus Christ into their soul-hearts as the Son of God, who redeemed us from the law of sin and death, now have the right to become children of God. "To believe" is to have unwavering faith. Notice John is acknowledging the legal right awarded believers in the Kingdom of God. As stated on the cross by Jesus himself, the penalties for our rebellions were paid once and for all when He stated, "It is finished" (John 19:30). In Colossians 2: 13 – 14 obtaining the legal right to be children of God is further described.

¹³And you, being dead in your trespasses and the uncircumcision of your flesh, He has made alive together with Him, having forgiven you all trespasses, ¹⁴having wiped out the handwriting of requirements that was against us, which was contrary to us. And He has taken it out of the way, having nailed it to the cross.

As explained in earlier chapters, living on the terms of this world order is outside of the harmony and order of God's Kingdom principles. While each one of us was still caught in this way of life, Jesus became the sin offering necessary to satisfy the legal requirement of heavenly justice and principles. Jesus' death and resurrection brought reconciliation between humanity and God's divine order. The handwriting that was wiped out was the record of rebellion of each individual in words and deeds recorded in heaven. The legal debt was paid and canceled in heavenly records. Every form of rebellion was nailed to the cross. Individual rights under the covenant of the blood of Jesus are given and recognized in the courts of heaven.

A legal contract between God and the person is completed when a person agrees to the terms of the contract. John states whoever believes and verbally agrees with the accomplishments of Jesus demonstrates evidence of accepting the contract to heavenly courts. Next, John also mentions the process of becoming children of God. This is the way of functioning within the bounds of the legal contract issued in heaven. He distinguishes this aspect by recognizing the individual's submission to the will of God. As mentioned in earlier chapters, it is an active surrender to the authority of God in one's life. These actions are born of daily commitment to the covenant of the blood of Jesus. Later in his book, John explains this process as being born of the Spirit rather than the will of man, to Nicodemus (John 3:1 -21). Modern Christianity describes being born again as:

> ➤ the acceptance and surrender to Jesus Christ as Lord
>
> ➤ the repenting and turning from an old lifestyle
>
> ➤ the entering of a new covenant with God through Jesus Christ

Growing into a fully mature child of God begins at this time. In the earthly realm, newborns trust and depend on parents to teach them how to live in their world. It is also true for newborn believers to be summitted to Father God's plans and authority to grow into full maturity in Christ Jesus. This is staying under the covenant of the blood of Jesus.

Thanks to our savior, Jesus Christ, we have been redeemed and reconciled to our God through his death and resurrection (Colossians 1:19 – 21). We have become heirs of our Father God as stated in Galatians 3:26

> *For you are all sons of God through faith in Christ Jesus.*

As noted in an earlier chapter, this beginning faith is the size of a mustard seed, and we enter this relationship with child-like understanding. We are to apply and develop this seed of faith. As explained previously, it is accomplished in submission. Surrender makes us teachable to that which is only learned through spirit-to-spirit communication. As we grow, applying faith and maturing in our spiritual bodies, we function at higher levels of understanding in the spiritual realm. As stated in Galatians 4:6 -7

> *⁶And because you are sons, God has sent forth the Spirit of His Son into your hearts, crying out, "Abba, Father!" ⁷Therefore you are no longer a slave but a son, and if a son, then an heir of God through Christ.*

Paul is alluding to being slaves to sin when we were under the laws of sin and death. We carry Christ's spirit in our bodies. When we cleanse our soul-hearts and build it on the word of God, our soul-hearts have intimate knowledge of Father God through Christ's spirit within us. The awakened soul-heart embraces sonship. Now spiritual organs such as eyes and ears begin to grow and function to know the spiritual terrain.

Think and Write about it

1. What does it mean to be born of the will of God? (John 1:12-14)

2. What spiritual tools do we use to grow the spiritual seed of faith and birth spiritual organs?

The practice of surrendering to God's will allows one to learn how to navigate within this spiritual body in the spiritual realm. The Holy Spirit teaches each person how to learn in this realm as stated in 1 John 2:27:

> *But the anointing which you have received from Him abides in you, and you do not need that anyone teach you; but as the same anointing teaches you concerning all things, and is true, and is not a lie, and just as it has taught you, you will abide in Him.*

Embracing sonship, spending greater time in intimate communication with God, and nourishing ourselves with God's words so they reside in our soul-hearts increases the ability for Jesus Christ to abide within us. Abiding in this manner is the first step to learning from the Holy Spirit. The practice of trusting Jesus Christ to abide in you builds structures in the spiritual realm within our soul/spirit bodies. Descriptions in the Bible of places become spiritual structures in our soul/spirit bodies. An example of this process is found when meditating on Psalm 18:2.

> *The LORD is my rock and my fortress and my deliverer; My God, my strength, in whom I will trust; My shield and the horn of my salvation, my stronghold.*

When we own this verse as our right as children of God, we build a stronghold in our spirit/soul bodies which resists fears and doubts. Our spiritual bodies pull by faith the spiritual substances from heaven into our soul-heart, grabbing and planting the truth in us. This structure, or stronghold now stands when we are assailed by fear. Trust is not in our own strength, wisdom, or any other abilities. Our trust and reliance are on God alone. Daily declarations like these, strengthen the walls of this spiritual stronghold as a right as heirs over the attacks of the enemy. When under attack by the enemy, we declare these truths. Just as Jesus demonstrated when the enemy attacked Him in the desert, we speak God's words in truth. This is done in full faith, without doubt or hesitation. We become single-minded and committed to God alone, avoiding double minded conditions as described in James 1:6 – 8.

> *⁶But let him ask in faith, with no doubting, for he who doubts is like a wave of the sea driven and tossed by the wind. ⁷For let not that man suppose that he will receive anything from the Lord; ⁸he is a double-minded man, unstable in all his ways.*

Paul summarizes the process of standing in truth about who a person is as a child of God in Romans 8:16 – 18:

> *16The Spirit Himself bears witness with our spirit that we are children of God, 17and if children, then heirs— heirs of God and joint heirs with Christ, if indeed we suffer with Him, that we may also be glorified together.*

The Holy Spirit in us agrees with our spirit bodies which claim the rights of the children of God. The witness supports the evidence recorded in the court of heaven. We are to know this proof and have written it in our soul-hearts that we are children of God. As children we declare the words of God as our own. By writing them on our soul-hearts we are possessing the words as our own. As we stand in faith, declaring God's words to his creation, we exercise our rights and responsibilities on earth. The Hoy Spirit then, is a witness to this proof in the spiritual realm. As we build truth within our soul-hearts and apply it to events in our lives, we demonstrate our authority under the legal contract with King Jesus as our Lord.

Think and Write about it

1. How does meditating on God's words build greater unity with God in spiritual realms?

2. How does the Holy Spirit assist us in developing our spiritual organs?

Privileges within the Kingdom of God are granted the heirs of King Jesus. We have through faith and spiritual actions built spiritual structures within our spirit/soul bodies. These structures are aligned with the Kingdom of God principles. The suffering Paul is referring to is crucifying ourselves with Christ as recorded in Galatians 2:20. The method of death of the old soul-heart was described in an earlier chapter. Jesus made it clear to his disciples that death of self was required when He described those who would serve Him as disciples under His Kingdom authority. As recorded in Luke 9:23:

> *Then He said to them all, "If anyone desires to come after Me, let him deny himself, and take up his cross daily, and follow Me.*

As children of God, we now have the privilege of being glorified with our King Jesus as co-heirs. We also have the responsibility to live a life in agreement with the

Kingdom of God principles. Privileges and responsibilities co-exist. As stated in 2 Corinthians 7:1:

> *Therefore, having these promises, beloved, let us cleanse ourselves from all filthiness of the flesh and spirit, perfecting holiness in the fear of God.*

To be glorified as mentioned above in Romans chapter eight requires spiritual work in the spiritual realm. When we honor Father God for who He is, we are doing that type of spiritual work. When we seek the Kingdom of God principles and surrender our wills to serve God under this authority, we are completing spiritual work. When we let go of our understanding and wisdom and align with all Jesus Christ is in our soul-hearts and soul-minds we are completing spiritual work. We agree for our old selves to be stripped away so that Jesus Christ can live deeper in our spirits. Jesus prayed for Father God to aid us in this process before going to the cross as recorded in John 17:17

> *"Sanctify them by Your truth. Your word is truth.*

The actions taken to accomplish this task is spiritual work. Even though we have the legal right to be children of God, Jesus is praying for His followers to commit to allowing the word of God to change them. By our own choice, we choose to apply the truths of the heavenly Kingdom to our three bodies to cleanse them.

In the same prayer, Jesus described God's purpose and intent for this type of surrender to the authority of Kingdom of God principles. As recorded in John 17:23

> *"I in them, and You in Me; that they may be made perfect in one, and that the world may know that You have sent Me, and have loved them as You have loved Me.*

Jesus was praying for his followers to know such unity with Him, that His holiness would find a home in our soul bodies. For Father God to enter this union with a believer and Jesus Christ, the sanctifying of one's body is necessary. It is what Jesus means when he states, "made perfect in one." He is praying for a process to happen as we submit to King Jesus as Lord of our lives. This is the hope of Glory Jesus had when he accomplished all He did from the Garden of Gethsemane through His ascension right before Pentecost (Colossians 1:27). We, the children of God, would mature in our spiritual relationship with God so we would be made perfect in Christ. We are to be His masterpieces displaying the absolute love of God to people in the earthly realm.

When we have surrendered to God's plan of salvation and yielded to the directions of the Holy Spirit, believers can enter into the process listed above and explained in previous chapters. Our goal is to be holy temples for our God to use to bring his divine purpose and order into what God created, our world. It is in humility and obedience, and not with our own wisdom this is accomplished. As stated in Philippians 2:12 - 13

> *12Therefore, my beloved, as you have always obeyed, not as in my presence only, but now much more in my absence, work out your own salvation with fear and trembling; 13for it is God who works in you both to will and to do for His good pleasure.*

We learn to be coworkers with God in our own salvation, stripping from our soul-hearts what Holy Spirit convicts us to destroy and planting God's words in our soul-hearts. We develop greater respect for God's ways and God's timing as we listen and obey Holy Spirit's directions. We learn to let God have His way in our lives. Waiting on God and then moving when the Holy Spirit directs us, teaches us the rhythm of heaven. It increases our sensitivity to spirit-to-spirit communication.

James explains how we learn God's ways and timing over our own understanding. As recorded in James 1:2 -5

> *2My brethren, count it all joy when you fall into various trials, 3knowing that the testing of your faith produces patience. 4But let patience have its perfect work, that you may be perfect and complete, lacking nothing. 5If any of you lacks wisdom, let him ask of God, who gives to all liberally and without reproach, and it will be given to him.*

Patience is the result of holding onto God's timing through the works of faith. James later states that trials are not of God's making (James 1:13 – 15). Trials come from an imperfect world, malformed by the enemy's influence on unredeemed people. In this imperfect world, the believers are to follow Paul's directions described in Philippians 2:12 - 13. We surrender to God who works with us as Paul stated to bring about the perfect solution.

James explains that what Jesus prayed is achieved in the process of surrender and working with God to overcome obstacles in this world. He recorded it in James 1: 12

> *Blessed is the man who endures temptation; for when he has been approved, he will receive the crown of life which the Lord has promised to those who love Him.*

Our greatest temptations are bred from pride and independence. These temptations call from the world's perspective to live life on our own terms. For believers it comes in the form of compromising God's words with the world's views. This is why submission to King Jesus and daily eating the word of God is so important. As stated by Paul, God leads us through the Holy Spirit to grow faith and spiritual bodies so we may embrace our inheritance as children of God (Philippians 2:12 – 13). We develop habits of dependency on God, bringing forth spiritual fruit. These habits also build spiritual structures in our spirit/soul bodies. We learn as we function as coworkers in alignment with Kingdom of God principles. We are cleansed and made holy through the ordained process of God.

It is time to do our part as coworkers with God to move into full maturity in Christ. As Paul stated in Philippians 3:13 – 14:

> *13Brethren, I do not count myself to have apprehended; but one thing I do, forgetting those things which are behind and reaching forward to those things which are ahead, 14I press toward the goal for the prize of the upward call of God in Christ Jesus.*

Paul is actively reaching into his own future. His spiritual eyes are on the final goal of complete unity in Christ as Jesus and brotherhood with believers is described in the prayer in John 17. His work centered upon bringing Gentiles into spiritual unity as believers with the Jewish believers, knowing Jesus Christ as Messiah. Unity with all people, through unity with Christ Jesus, was Paul's goal. He became single minded, not allowing anything to stop or hinder this goal. Paul, who first persecuted believers, understood John 17:20 -21:

> *20"I do not pray for these alone, but also for those who will believe in Me through their word; 21that they all may be one, as You, Father, are in Me, and I in You; that they also may be one in Us, that the world may believe that You sent Me.*

The goal of mature Sons and Daughters of God is unity in God and unity with our spiritual family members. Salvation is not simply for oneself. We died to self so King Jesus would rise in us. As Jesus stated in the great commission (Mathew 28:18 – 20), we are to be ambassadors of God's Kingdom to those who are perishing in chains of darkness in an imperfect world. We are to move into our world demonstrating the love of God. Mature children of God are to disciple others to enter the Kingdom of God.

Think and Write about it

1. What are our spiritual responsibilities as children of God?

2. How do we learn to apply the rhythm of heaven to our lives?

3. How does surrendering to God's will overcome the temptations and trials from the world?

In One Accord

One of the biggest roadblocks for western believers is the western cultural understanding of the power of the individual. Within the western church, too much emphasis is placed on personal growth rather than unity in Jesus Christ just as the Father God and Jesus Christ are one. Yes, each person comes to salvation by stating agreement with the heavenly contract through the blood of Jesus. Unfortunately, western thinking keeps people in a mindset that opposes the intent of God to create tribes of families in His kingdom on earth. God intended all believers to be one in spirit and purpose under His authority. No recognition of position in society was to taint the unity through faith in Jesus Christ as Lord. As stated in Galatians 3:26 – 28:

> *26For you are all sons of God through faith in Christ Jesus. 27For as many of you as were baptized into Christ have put on Christ. 28There is neither Jew nor Greek, there is neither slave nor free, there is neither male nor female; for you are all one in Christ Jesus.*

A mature believer moves past self into a personal relationship with God and into mutually respectful relationship with brothers and sisters in Christ. Both of these types of love are required by God as evidence of believers abiding in Jesus Christ. As Stated in 1 John 3:14 – 15

> *14We know that we have passed from death to life because we love the brethren. He who does not love his brother abides in death. 15Whoever hates his brother is a murderer, and you know that no murderer has eternal life abiding in him.*

Strong words from Apostle John are given here! Jesus Christ may abide in us. We may participate in the advantage of the legal contract in heaven. This is Jesus Christ dwelling in us. For us to abide in Jesus Christ as well, is a demonstration of a greater surrender of self. When we quit weighing the advantage of completing tasks for personal gain or loss, we begin this last stage of surrender of self. The unity God is seeking takes love for another as a willing choice even when it is inconvenient and involving personal sacrifice. Our spiritual eyes are not only to be on Jesus but also on those who serve Him. This combination of love for God and building with others in love brings the bending of self into a family of believers. Without the love and respect of other believers, the church becomes a club. As stated in Romans 12:10:

Be kindly affectionate to one another with brotherly love, in honor giving preference to one another...

As noted earlier, sanctifying oneself to be stripped of self-centered focus is one of the indications of Jesus Christ living in the new believer. Jesus Christ abiding in us is nurtured through an intimate personal relationship with God. Yet stopping at this stage is like the tribes of Israel who stopped on the desert side of the Jordan River. In their minds they had sacrificed enough and what they now possessed was better than before. They were no longer slaves and had freedom to live as God intended. It was enough of God for them to continue to live their lives in this world. They weighed the cost of crossing over and fighting giants to live in the promised land and decided it was too great a sacrifice.

God intends to have a spotless bride for His son, King Jesus (Ephesians 5:27). This bride, His church, will function in unity of one mind, one heart, one will, and one spirit under the authority of Kingdom of Heaven principles. As recorded in Philippians 2:1 -2:

> *[1]Therefore if there is any consolation in Christ, if any comfort of love, if any fellowship of the Spirit, if any affection and mercy, [2]fulfill my joy by being like-minded, having the same love, being of one accord, of one mind.*

Though we are individually held accountable to God for every word and action committed while we live on earth, it is in unity the mature children of God accomplish the work of the Kingdom of God on earth. In gratitude for what the grace of God has given each individual and the pouring of God's love into us, we are to seek like-minded, spirit-filled people. Paul's next sentence in Philippians warns of what not to do as individuals. Philippians 2:3

> *Let nothing be done through selfish ambition or conceit, but in lowliness of mind let each esteem others better than himself.*

As we move from Christ living in us to us abiding in Christ, selfish ambition is to die. Working with others in unity is not to be tainted by pride or ownership of the work. Conceit always carries a form of judging others and pride. God pours His love in us, so we know God. God is love (1 John 4:16). We are not simply to be a sponge, soaking up the gift of love for our own pleasures. This love is the binding between others and us. Many of those who are brought together possess different ways and means of living. Christ is the head of the church, and His followers are to unite as a body (Ephesians 1:22).

Think and Write about it

1. When we abide in Jesus Christ, we are to seek greater union with our tribe of Christians. What does this look like in your life? Do you see any areas which the Holy Spirit would like to refine in this area?

2. What are two individual attitudes that interfere with building corporate unity in Christ?

Jesus told His disciples of a Kingdom of God principle concerning the unity of believers. As recorded in Matthew 18:19 – 20:

> [19]*"Again I say to you that if two of you agree on earth concerning anything that they ask, it will be done for them by My Father in heaven.* [20]*"For where two or three are gathered together in My name, I am there in the midst of them."*

Individuals should pray in their prayer closets and seek God. It is part of continually building a personal relationship with God. Jesus even told His followers God will give gifts to His followers who ask (Mathew 7:11). The Kingdom of God principle Jesus is describing in these verses concerning prayer is how God's government is to operate within the earthly realm. Under covenant principles, believers have the responsibility and authority to align with God's heavenly Kingdom. They also have the responsibility under covenant to possess the spiritual landscape and occupy it. The method of calling into the physical realm the plans, authority, and purpose of God's heavenly Kingdom is through agreement with like-minded people. This is why we are to not only have Jesus abide in us, but we are also to abide in Him. To bring alignment between the Kingdom of God and the body of Christ, the people are to be one in spirit, mind, heart, and will. It is through Jesus this alignment occurs as He recognizes those who are in Him. Jesus enters the midst of the gathering of His people. The head and body can then complete the work of bringing the Kingdom of God into the earthly realm to declare and rule.

John identifies a crucial piece for this unity to accomplish the will of God on earth. We are to love one another as Jesus loved us (John 15:12). Brotherly love is crucial to alignment with Kingdom of God principles, as John states in 1 John 4: 20 – 21:

²⁰If someone says, "I love God," and hates his brother, he is a liar; for he who does not love his brother whom he has seen, how can he love God whom he has not seen? ²¹And this commandment we have from Him: that he who loves God must love his brother also.

To function under the Kingdom of God principles as rulers within the earth, unity in brotherly love is crucial. There is one King, Jesus, and one body in Him and under His authority. Believers in King Jesus as Lord are rulers under King Jesus' authority and subject to obedience to Holy Spirit directions. Two or three cannot call Jesus into the midst of their prayers and praise without unity and submission to the will of God. Holy Spirit is the strategist who coordinates how the will of God is to be implemented in prayer and declaration. Jesus made that clear to His disciples. We are to abide in Jesus as He abides in us (John 15:10). Then when two or three come together in one spirit, one mind and one heart, in obedience to Kingdom principles, Jesus will be with us.   The words declared in the Lord's prayer will be lived by His bride. "Thy Kingdom come as it is in heaven" will be lived and declared by this bride. To dwell in Jesus Christ as He dwells in us is the greater abiding in God. Proof of both types of love, love for God and love for others are required for the mature son and daughter of God. Jesus Himself made this clear as recorded in John 15:12:

"This is My commandment, that you love one another as I have loved you."

To love as Jesus did is a tall order. This love is full of mercy, grace, and forgiveness. Now Apostle John's words make more sense. Following Jesus' commandments is how we show evidence of being children of God (John 14:23). This is proof that we, mature believers, are abiding in Jesus (John 15:9 – 10).

If we return now to 1 John 3:14 - 15, we now can understand how the degree of our love for our brethren affects operating within the Kingdom of God principles.

¹⁴We know that we have passed from death to life, because we love the brethren. He who does not love his brother abides in death. ¹⁵Whoever hates his brother is a murderer, and you know that no murderer has eternal life abiding in him.

Death is a product of chaos and rebellion. As noted earlier, those who truly love God and abide in Him have destroyed this root of sin, which is chaos and rebellion. The blood of Jesus applied through faith overcomes and destroys this root. Only life can be found in the believer who lives in this faith. At the spiritual level, we who believe know we have passed from death's authority and power into life through this covenant with God. Apostle John clarifies how the level of love Jesus possessed for His followers is measured. If we do not love our brothers, we are rebelling against Jesus Christ's commandments. We have brought the source of death and rebellion, into our soul bodies. We have contaminated what God has made holy by the blood of Jesus. We cannot rise further into Jesus Christ when our soul bodies contain roots of both life and death. The promises of us abiding in Jesus are only fulfilled when we move into greater surrender. Before we embrace greater love for believers, Jesus still abides in us. The Holy Spirit still directs us in how to overcome this death source in us. John makes it clear the solution is owning and living under Jesus' commandment to love the children of God as he did. John draws a distinction between not loving a brother and hating one. The extreme of hating a brother is akin to murdering a brother. It is embracing roots of sin, rebellion, and chaos, and allowing it to overcome a soul-heart. This act brings death to the cleansed soul-heart, poisoning it with rebellion to God's Kingdom principles. On the other hand, not loving a brother poisons a heart with numerous possible sins that can be renounced, loosened from a soul-heart, and forgiven. Jealousy, offense, judgmental superior attitudes, and blame are just a few of the possible attitudes that interfere with brotherly love. As noted in earlier chapters, all of these can be taken to the cross. The attitudes can be removed and forgiven. John recognizes a continuum from not accepting and loving another believer to hating the person. The answer in God's created world is love conquers all. As stated in 1 Corinthians 13:9, Love never fails. Loving God and loving fellow believers will destroy every root of rebellion and chaos.

Think and Write about it

1. Why is it necessary for believers to come together to accomplish Kingdom of God government?

Living in Brotherly Love

The Bible defines how we are to demonstrate our love for our brothers and sisters in Christ Jesus. It is summarized in Galatians 6:10

Therefore, as we have opportunity, let us do good to all, especially to those who are of the household of faith.

Our spiritual definition of good comes from God (Mark 10:18). It is one of God's attributes. We know what is good by God's actions toward us. Jesus Christ is the embodiment of God (Hebrews 1:3). Through the way Jesus lived His life, we know what "good" is. Believers who submit to the authority of King Jesus gain the ability to function as Jesus Christ did through faith and obedience. As mentioned in an earlier chapter, we may act by living through the mind of Christ. Just as Jesus did, we listen for the voice of God in the form of the Holy Spirit. We submit and obey His directions. As Peter described it in 1 Peter 1:22 - 23:

²²Since you have purified your souls in obeying the truth through the Spirit in sincere love of the brethren, love one another fervently with a pure heart, ²³having been born again, not of corruptible seed but incorruptible, through the word of God which lives and abides forever...

The Bible further guides what actions and attitudes toward the family of God are acceptable and what is to be avoided. The written word of God combined with direction from the Holy Spirit sets parameters about how to love as Jesus did.

Love is the center of the Kingdom of God principles. It is alive in the spiritual realm and from God. It is in loving God, for all He accomplished in our lives, we enter into a dependent, loving relationship with our Lord God. Thus, it is in applying this love for God we can seek unity with other believers. As stated in 1 Thessalonians 3:12 – 13:

¹²And may the Lord make you increase and abound in love to one another and to all, just as we do to you, ¹³so that He may establish your hearts blameless in holiness before our God and Father at the coming of our Lord Jesus Christ with all His saints.

It is not in our own abilities we can achieve this love for one another. It is an act of faith. We depend on the Holy Spirit to convict us of what is still in us that built walls in our soul-hearts and soul-minds that supports division among our family of believers. We begin with listening more and talking less, as noted in James 1:19 – 20:

¹⁹So then, my beloved brethren, let every man be swift to hear, slow to speak, slow to wrath; ²⁰for the wrath of man does not produce the righteousness of God.

As we have learned to listen to the Holy Spirit for directions in our lives, we develop patience. We slow down our actions and check what is God's direction for us. In the same manner, when applying brotherly love to members of God's family, listening is key. It takes our mind away from our own agenda. It forces us to seek common ground, rather than waiting to impose our own solutions to common situations. Wrath is born out of seeking one's own way. It also comes in the form of offense when people believe their opinions and worth are not honored. Listening carefully to others helps reduce building ground for wrath. Humbling oneself while listening for the Holy Spirit's directions when interacting with other believers is rising in spiritual truth. It is acting in faith when seeking unity in brotherly love.

Acceptance of others builds unity. Not all people who are family in the body of Christ are functioning at the same spiritual level. Each person grows in faith. As Paul notes in Romans 14:1(NIV)

Accept the one whose faith is weak, without quarreling over disputable matters.

Grace is extending time, love, and patience to another as they grow in wisdom and understanding in one's relationship with God. True grace is not being a stumbling block for the growth in faith of other believers. Holy Spirit convicts each of us of what is truth. We are to allow others to have opportunities to grow, and we are not to judge their measure of faith. This section of Romans dealt with a common dispute over religion's traditional answers for eating food. It was a tradition of humanity about what is acceptable to eat. Unfortunately, it is still a doubtful tradition. A similar one would be how someone celebrates Christmas or Easter with family traditions. Doubt-filled disputes are ways one justifies one's behavior, focusing on the earthly actions rather than abiding in Christ. Another is related to healing. We stand in faith that Jesus is our healer. It is our faith that calls this healing forward into our physical bodies. There are various methods God uses to answer this call to faith and healing. The family of God is not to be a stumbling block to others in their faith understanding. When one becomes adamant about only one way faith can be applied, it is judgmental. We are to honor that is it God who raises Jesus Christ in us. It takes time for a believer to move into maturity. We, the body of Christ do not have the right to stand over others and determine if their walk with God is faithful enough. It is a faith walk in surrender each person makes with God. We are to submit and trust the Holy Spirit to bring each of us in alignment with God's will.

Paul's warning of disrupting unity in Christ's body is to the one who insists on one's own understanding being the one and only pathway in areas of dispute not delineated in the Bible. Please understand, this is not directed toward what is clearly a principle of God's Kingdom and covenant, but rather Paul is addressing human tradition. The issue is how we allow the spirit of disunity to enter our midst as the body of believers. As stated in Romans 14:4:

Who are you to judge another's servant? To his own master he stands or falls. Indeed, he will be made to stand, for God is able to make him stand.

We are equal servants of God. We are answerable to our God for our actions toward others. God's anger is at the demons that created the lies that separate people from Him. Nor are we to judge another person's actions that the church labels as sin. We do not know the soul-hearts of others. We all stand before God. As noted in James 2:13

For judgment is without mercy to the one who has shown no mercy. Mercy triumphs over judgment.

For God gives mercy to people caught in darkness and traps of His enemy. When we accepted Jesus as Lord, while we were still caught in darkness, we still carried the seeds of rebellion in our souls. Mercy is one of the essences of God. We, His body, are not to place our understanding above God's mercy. This mercy withholds all blame and delays the harvest of seeds planted in rebellion. If we act from the mind of Christ, we have lined our soul-hearts and soul-minds with mercy. Not by our actions are we returned to right relationship with God. Rather it is God's grace. All who are called to be the body of Christ on earth have the same entry, grace. Only Jesus Christ has the right to judge. It is not our place to determine if a fellow believer is walking in truth with God. As noted in Romans 14:10:

> *But why do you judge your brother? Or why do you show contempt for your brother? For we shall all stand before the judgment seat of Christ.*

The way of love is acceptance, patience, and grace. It is found in James' admonishment to be slow to speak and quick to listen. We all received our redemption through grace, not actions on our own part. We do not have the right to judge anyone. Our righteousness was bought at the price of the blood of the Son of God. Since all who are called into unity in the body of Christ have the same righteousness, we cannot judge and build roadblocks in our soul-hearts and soul-minds against others. For ultimately, any roadblocks built to cover our soul-hearts are against God and feed rebellion.

When our goal is to be one in Christ and to abide in Him as He abides in us, we trust the Holy Spirit to lead others as we have been led. Our confidence is in Jesus Christ alone. As Paul states in Romans 14:7 – 8:

> *[7]For none of us lives to himself, and no one dies to himself. [8]For if we live, we live to the Lord; and if we die, we die to the Lord. Therefore, whether we live or die, we are the Lord's.*

We no longer have a life of our own. The old has passed away and we are a new creation, bought and paid for with the blood of Jesus (2 Corinthians 5:17). We are to trust the Holy Spirit who teaches us all. We rise in faith, following where the Holy Spirit directs us. We pray for our eyes of understanding to open to know how to interact with our spiritual family. We pray blessings on other spiritual family members. Then we trust what is written in Romans 15:5 – 6:

> *[5]Now may the God of patience and comfort grant you to be like-minded toward one another, according to Christ Jesus, [6]that you may with one mind and one mouth glorify the God and Father of our Lord Jesus Christ.*

Comfort and patience are given through grace in our God. Leaning deeper into Him during our prayer closet times will give us the strength and wisdom about how to live in peace with our spiritual family in Christ as one body.

Think and Write about it

1. What is our standard for determining how to act in brotherly love?

2. What is true grace in relationships with fellow believers?

3. What are some examples of being a stumbling block to someone else's growing faith? When have you been a stumbling block?

Peter called for the believers to follow a pattern to support brotherly love within the body of Christ. As stated in 1 Peter 3:8 – 9:

> [8]*Finally, all of you be of one mind, having compassion for one another; love as brothers, be tenderhearted, be courteous;* [9]*not returning evil for evil or reviling for reviling, but on the contrary blessing, knowing that you were called to this, that you may inherit a blessing.*

He is agreeing with James when he states we are to be courteous, or respectful of others. As tenderhearted people, we are to interact with each other by extending mercy. Pour love into others when spending time with them. We are to bless one another. As mentioned earlier, we begin this process in our intimate time with God in our prayer closets. Actions follow seeking God's wisdom. Peter further warns of what not to do in relationship with fellow believers. When attacked, judged, put down, or isolated by the actions of other believers, we are not to treat them in the same manner. Again, walking in faith as we abide in Jesus means focusing on spiritual truths, not earthly actions. When we operate in the mind of Christ, we are abiding in Him. Jesus was betrayed by Judas, a disciple whom He loved. Yes, even though He knew the truth in the heart of Judas, Jesus never called him out. Jesus applied mercy in his relationship with Judas. He trusted God's timing to fulfill the prophecies. If we are to abide in Christ, we follow His pattern of pouring more forgiveness into those who choose not to act in love toward us. In our spirit bodies we rise up and claim the words recorded in 1 Thessalonians 3:12 -13 (NIV):

> *12May the Lord make your love increase and overflow for each other and for everyone else, just as ours does for you. 13May he strengthen your hearts so that you will be blameless and holy in the presence of our God and Father when our Lord Jesus comes with all his holy ones.*

In our own strength we cannot rise above the circumstances. Our source of love is God. If we are not to carry guilt, anger, shame, blame, and regret from interactions with others, we need to trust God in greater measure. We are to forgive. Only through God's love poured into us can we surrender hurts to the true source of forgiveness. More love is the only answer to overcome the plans of the enemy to cause disunity in the bride of Christ. It is not in our own strength this is accomplished, but rather God's.

Later Paul expands this principle with a Kingdom of God principle. As recorded in 1 Thessalonians 4: 6 – 7 (NIV)

> *…6and that in this matter no one should wrong or take advantage of a brother or sister. The Lord will punish all those who commit such sins, as we told you and warned you before. 7For God did not call us to be impure, but to live a holy life.*

The principle of seedtime, growth time and harvest time is active in the life of all believers. So is God's mercy and grace. Again, we do not know the hearts of those that attack us. Only God knows the plans He has for them. To step into the process of what God is accomplishing in the life of another by operating from the physical worldview is raising one's position to that of the Holy Spirit. We are not acting in faith from our spiritual minds, but rather from traditions of humanity that have polluted our soul-hearts. We then bring the judgment on ourselves by being the stumbling block for the work of God. God's word points to the results of this approach with fellow believers in Hebrews 12:15:

> *…looking carefully lest anyone fall short of the grace of God; lest any root of bitterness springing up cause trouble, and by this many become defiled…*

We are to trust grace. Grace is one of God's forms. We know grace overcomes all sins (Romans 5:20). For it is through grace we are accepted into right relationship with

God. Allow grace to work in the bride of Christ through the Holy Spirit, not our tainted soul-hearts.

This warning is further developed by James. As recorded in James 4:11 – 12 (NIV):

> *[11]Brothers and sisters, do not slander one another. Anyone who speaks against a brother or sister or judges them speaks against the law and judges it. When you judge the law, you are not keeping it, but sitting in judgment on it. [12]There is only one Lawgiver and Judge, the one who is able to save and destroy. But you—who are you to judge your neighbor?*

Mature believers in Jesus Christ as Lord not only have Jesus abiding in them but they abide in Jesus. Those who are pulled into slander and judgment have not accomplished what Jesus required of His followers. Mathew 7:1 - 2 records Jesus stating:

> *[1]Judge not, that you be not judged. [2]For with what judgment you judge, you will be judged; and with the measure you use, it will be measured back to you.*

Believers who honor Jesus commands are the ones Jesus states love him. He abides in them. When we love as Jesus did, we abide in Jesus. It is only through more love for God and more surrender to God a person moves into abiding in Jesus.

In the same manner, God's words warn of preferring one believer over another. As recorded in James 2:1 (NIV)

> *My brothers and sisters, believers in our glorious Lord Jesus Christ must not show favoritism.*

When a believer operates from the mind of Christ, the rules and honors of the world do not hold value in the soul-heart of the believer. All of us, from every walk of life, bring into our beginning relationship with Jesus the misunderstandings of social order into our time of fellowship. This is to be broken on the altars as we cleanse our soul-hearts. James further explains this in James 2:8 – 9 (NIV)

> *[8]If you really keep the royal law found in Scripture, "Love your neighbor as yourself," you are doing right. [9]But if you show favoritism, you sin and are convicted by the law as lawbreakers.*

In other words, the transgression is poisoning one's soul-heart with a root of rebellion. A believer cannot move in greater unity with Jesus Christ when both the root of life and the root of death occupy the soul-heart. Again, those who are to abide in Jesus are to follow all His commandments. It is demonstrated in love. Preference for one over another reflects the world's perspective and waters down the love God wants to flow in His bride. The enemy's design is to mix worldly traditions into the bride of Christ. Through old habits of judging others on social scales, division enters the body of Christ. Any form of judgment not taken to the personal prayer closets of individual members defiles the body of Christ. Keeping our eyes focused on our Lord Jesus allows us to walk in faith. Time spent with the Holy Spirit convicts each person of anything that defiles the unity the Holy Spirit is building in the bride of Christ.

Think and Write about it

1. What actions between believers demonstrate they are functioning in one accord?

2. How does first loving God help the family of God to love each other?

As noted in Peter's first letter, we are the building blocks within the body of Christ. As recorded in 1 Peter 2: 3 – 5:

> …*3if indeed you have tasted that the Lord is gracious. 4Coming to Him as to a living stone, rejected indeed by men, but chosen by God and precious, 5you also, as living stones, are being built up a spiritual house, a holy priesthood, to offer up spiritual sacrifices acceptable to God through Jesus Christ.*

Those of us who have accepted the grace of God, to enter into relationship with God through Jesus Christ, the living cornerstone of the Blood Covenant, are called by God. We now live under that covenant, renewed, transformed, and built up in Christ. As we become united with the mind and heart of Christ, we abide in Him. As we submit to God's plans, He uses us to be the building blocks for His church, the bride of Christ. In submission to the Holy Spirit's guidance, we use the gifts given to us to be formed into this bride (1Peter 4:10).

As Jesus stated, we demonstrate our love to God by obeying all Jesus taught us. As recorded in Hebrews 10: 24 – 25:

> *24And let us consider one another in order to stir up love and good works, 25not forsaking the assembling of ourselves together, as is the manner of some, but exhorting one another, and so much the more as you see the Day approaching.*

Assembling as one body under the authority of Jesus Christ allows us to enter God's throne room in praise. When the people enter in one accord, then the business of the Kingdom of God can be accomplished while we are in our physical bodies on this earth. In this unity of one mind, one heart and one spirit we can call into this earth the Kingdom of God principles. As with all of the Kingdom of God principles, there are protocols to follow.

Praise is the beginning key to entering the presence of God. Jesus taught this in the Lord's prayer. David records it in numerous psalms. Every prayer of thanksgiving listed in the Old Testament starts with honoring God for who He is. It is also a declaration of who we are in relationship to our God. To seek the creator, one is to acknowledge our relationship to Him. In unity we submit to His authority and power through praise. Jesus stated we are to ask in His presence. It is only through Jesus we have the right to enter the throne room of God. As recorded in Hebrews 13:15 - 16:

> *15Therefore by Him let us continually offer the sacrifice of praise to God, that is, the fruit of our lips, giving thanks to His name. 16But do not forget to do good and to share, for with such sacrifices God is well pleased.*

Once in this atmosphere, submitted to the authority of God, the King's business can be conducted. Our assignment as the bride of Christ is to bring God's will into this earth and manifest the Kingdom of God in earthly realms. Kingdom business can include things for individuals as well as nations. James records one such action in James 5:16:

> *Confess your trespasses to one another, and pray for one another, that you may be healed. The effective, fervent prayer of a righteous man avails much.*

Confession and repentance are tools God gives His people to align with His Kingdom. We, the bride of Christ, can stand in the gap for others as well as nations for sins committed against God. We can plead for our advocate, Jesus Christ, to accept confessions as an offering of repentance. We can call forth healing for individuals using our faith to pull down God's righteousness into our mist. We can ask King Jesus, the Lord of the Hosts, to send His angels to fight for us against our common enemy, all anti-Christ spirits. We can ask these hosts of heaven to destroy strongholds built against our sovereign King Jesus to hold back God's people. In unity we can love each other as Christ loved his followers. As recorded in 1 Peter 4:8:

> *And above all things have fervent love for one another, for "love will cover a multitude of sins."*

Our God founded our existence and our world in love. He redeemed it with acts of love through Jesus Christ. God sent the Holy Spirit to direct us to become the bride of Christ as we surrender to being re-formed as individuals and then joined through faith and love. As we stand united in Christ, we are to declare and bring the Kingdom of God principles into our earth. It is accomplished through love.

Think and Write about it

1. Explain the pattern God ordained to assemble His people to complete God's actions in the earthly realm?

2. What is the protocol for entering in the Spirit into God's presence?

5

Master, Teach Us to Pray

As the disciples watched Jesus perform miracles, teach scripture with new revelation, attack storms, and cast out demons from people, there was one thing they asked. Teach us to pray as you do (Luke 11:1). On one level they knew Jesus' foundation for wisdom and revelation and how Jesus accomplished these tasks, was grounded in Jesus' intimate relationship with Father God. Every time Jesus was confronted by religious authorities he had one defense. He only did what Father God told Him to speak and do (John 5:19 & John 6:38). Though this intimate relationship had been seen in other patriarchs in Jewish history, the opportunity to gain firsthand wisdom had not existed for over four hundred years. Regularly, the disciples saw Jesus leave their company to go alone to pray to God. A key to all they were witnessing existed in the intimate relationship with God and the manner Jesus approached Father God. So they asked for a pattern on how to do the same. Thus, what is known as the Lord's Prayer was birthed.

When the Lord's Prayer is examined as a process answer to a question about how to approach God and be intimate with Him, hidden revelation flows from the words. Through rote usage of the prayer, the revelation has been buried. It is more than a pattern of how to pray. The revelation only comes alive when the seeker of God is searching for an intimate relationship with God. On the other side of the cross and resurrection of Jesus Christ, the seeker finds a single doorway to God. The doorway is Jesus Christ, the risen Lord. Jesus told his disciples this before His crucifixion as recorded in John 10:9

> *"I am the door. If anyone enters by Me, he will be saved, and will go in and out and find pasture.*

Jesus told them again as recorded in John 14:6

> *Jesus said to him, "I am the way, the truth, and the life. No one comes to the Father except through Me.*

When the seeker of God submits to Jesus Christ as Lord, turning away from a former lifestyle, a pathway into an intimate relationship with God is opened. Now scripture comes alive. As 2 Timothy 3:16 - 17 states:

> *[16]All Scripture is given by inspiration of God, and is profitable for doctrine, for reproof, for correction, for instruction in righteousness, [17]that the man of God may be complete, thoroughly equipped for every good work.*

The words of the Lord's prayer are scripture. As Paul noted, these words are for instruction in righteousness.

The first verse of the Lord's prayer, "Our Father in heaven, hallowed be Your name" (Matthew 6:9), is a surrender and acknowledgment of who God is. By acknowledging God as Father, one is aligning oneself to the Creator as the source of one's existence. It is honoring the fact that each person comes from God. It is accepting the role as child. A child is dependent and a learner. A child turns to the father for instruction and correction to gain wisdom. There is submission to the authority of God when one is a child of God. A promise of an inheritance also rests in the acknowledgment of God as Father. This verse is then a declaration of submission of one's will to the authority of God.

Think and Write about it

1. Consider the role of a father. Take a few minutes and remember examples of when you experienced God in the following roles for you:

   A. Protector

   B. Provider

   C. Teacher

   D. Authority

   E. Defender

2. Now describe how you honor or hallow God. How often does this occur in your week? Do you recognize God's authority in your family? Your business dealings? Your friendships? Your leisure times? Give examples from your experience of when you have accomplished this. How would an outsider recognize your behavior as different from someone who does not honor God?

By declaring heaven as existing and being the home of God, a person recognizes a difference between earth and heaven. Heaven is acknowledged as a real place. It has substance created by God to maintain it. God is noted as a living being occupying a space that humanity does not. God is greater than what He has created. It is admitting the unseen heaven is also greater and more power-filled than the seen earthly realm. In the declaration, the seeker is stating one comes from a place outside of our earthly existence where the Being who creates lives and functions. Relationship with a greater being in another place is noted. One is declaring dependency on the being of God in heaven for life, support, and wisdom to grow into an inheritance from the older family member. When the seeker owns these truths as they are declared in the beginning of the Lord's Prayer, a proper respect for God is accomplished. It is the starting point of seeking God.

Think and Write about it

1. What is new in this revelation in declaring heaven as God's dwelling place?

A seeker's relationship with God is defined in this first statement. God, Creator, exists in another realm. From this other realm, God placed humanity in a different realm that God created. Furthermore, the seeker identifies there are two existing places or realms. One is dependent on the other for life and continuation of life. Heaven is the greater realm for it is the source of all life. God is hallowed or set apart to be holy from all His creation. He is pure in form or the original from which all else is derived. As beings that were created, a loyalty to what is our source of life is required. Honor, respect, and gratitude are just some of the expected responses from humanity. Praising the Creator is the proper response to express the right relationship between the created and the Creator. When this loyalty is not acknowledged, it places the humans in rebellion against Creator God and the system that supports humanity.

Creator God determined to give humanity free will. God intended for humanity to be his offspring (Hebrews 2:11 - 13). Humanity was to grow in relationship and become the likeness of God (Genesis 1:26). The ability to choose gives people ownership of their decisions and actions. Choices have consequences. Since Creator God designed the realm in which humanity lives, God chose how to balance and keep it in harmony. As stated in Romans 9:20

> *But indeed, O man, who are you to reply against God? Will the thing formed say to him who formed it, "Why have you made me like this?"*

In other words, the rules governing existence are God's. Blessing for those who operate within the bounds of this system as well as problems for those who work outside of the divine order are God's to mete out. Thus, choosing to grow in God's likeness was made a true option. The alternative is to be disloyal to God and live outside the order of creation. This is choosing chaos and eventually death. Choices have outcomes and consequences.

God's word gives clear statement of these options throughout the Bible. One place this is done is in Deuteronomy 30:19 – 20.

> *[19]I call heaven and earth as witnesses today against you, that I have set before you life and death, blessing and cursing; therefore choose life, that both you and your descendants may live; [20]that you may love the LORD your God, that you may obey His voice, and that you may cling to Him, for He is your life and the length of your days; and that you may dwell in the land which the LORD swore to your fathers, to Abraham, Isaac, and Jacob, to give them.*

Disobedience and disloyalty are signs that people do not love God. Whenever people are dishonoring God, they participate in actions that destroy harmony in the created order and chaos is the result. Rebellious people become self-serving and self-focused rather than God focused. Life is crippled in disorder; chaos rips protective systems and death follows. The results are in the hands of humanity. As God stated in Genesis (Genesis1:28) and later Jesus Christ confirmed, humans are responsible for maintaining life through harmony with God. After His resurrection, Jesus gave His disciples this assignment as recorded in Matthew 28:18:

¹⁸And Jesus came and spoke to them, saying, "All authority has been given to Me in heaven and on earth. ¹⁹Go therefore and make disciples of all the nations, baptizing them in the name of the Father and of the Son and of the Holy Spirit, ²⁰teaching them to observe all things that I have commanded you; and lo, I am with you always, even to the end of the age." Amen.

Creator God reconciled the heavens and earthly realm through the death, resurrection, and ascension of Jesus Christ (Colossians 1:19). All authority is in the hands of Jesus Christ. Nothing is greater or has move power than Jesus Christ. No created entity in the earthly realm or heavenly realms can overcome the authority of Jesus. Jesus appointed His disciples to be His representatives of this authority. The followers of Jesus are assigned to teach God's ways, as exemplified by Jesus Christ, and to align with the divine created order. Life is maintained by following this pattern.

Think and Write about it

How do the choices I make affect the harmony of life within the earth?

Kingdom of God

The next verse in the prayer is recorded in Mathew 6:10:

Your kingdom come. Your will be done On earth as it is in heaven.

Kingdom is more than a place. It is a system of government. A government contains rules of order, as well as checks and balances, to allow the realms to function in perfect order. In this case, what maintains life itself follows a created pattern and order. The mind of God created this pattern. Since the removal of Adam from the Garden of Eden, we, God's creation, now know about life and death. We know the difference between what is organic, living, moving, and functioning well and what is decay and death. In God there is life, and we come from this life. Outside of the order and rule of God there is disorder, chaos, and what we know as death. When we declare, "Your Kingdom come," we God's creation, are aligning with the original order and pattern of creation in the heavenly realm. In calling God's Kingdom forward into the earthly Kingdom there is a recognition that the earthly realm is in disorder. We are declaring our choice to align with the Creator and His patterns and not the disorder within the earthly realm. It is truly a declaration of war!

This declaration is further cemented with the statement, "Your will be done." Whose will is being overridden? First of all, it is the person declaring whose will is submitted to God's will. The seekers are stating while aligning with the heavenly Kingdom principles, they are subjugating their choices, behaviors, and attitudes beneath that of God's will. This is an enlistment into the army of God. All actions are to be submitted to God for approval before they are taken. As in any military operation, the combatant is to train daily. This is done in the prayer closets of believers.

The second will that is being overcome is the will of the enemy of God as expressed in worldly systems. The source of death and chaos in the earthly realm is rebellion to the order and will of God. James 4:4 explains is as follows:

> *Adulterers and adulteresses! Do you not know that friendship with the world is enmity with God? Whoever therefore wants to be a friend of the world makes himself an enemy of God.*

The word *"adulterers"* is hard. It implies that a person is leaving a covenant relationship and seeking pleasure and satisfaction outside of what one made as a commitment to honor. It is turning against their own sworn words given in the presence of God. As noted earlier, when created beings recognize their source of life is outside of themselves and this limited earthly realm, loyalty to the source of life is required. Rebellion against this truth creates disorder, chaos, and death. Seeking after the results of this rebellion is turning from life and embracing death. It is loving and desiring what will destroy life. The word *adultery* does describe the intent and the actions. Again, seeking God's will is a declaration of war!

Those who have chosen King Jesus as their Lord are being called out of the world's view and world order to change the atmosphere of the earthly realm. Their enlistment pledge was given as a covenant promise with King Jesus as Lord. As stated in Romans 10:9 – 10:

> *…⁹that if you confess with your mouth the Lord Jesus and believe in your heart that God has raised Him from the dead, you will be saved. ¹⁰For with the heart one believes unto righteousness, and with the mouth confession is made unto salvation.*

The soul-heart surrenders one's will to the authority of King Jesus. As mentioned earlier, the soul-heart is a place of foundational beliefs and attitudes. It is a compass to interpret events and impressions happening in a person's life. So, the truth of Jesus is written on the heart-soul, emboldening faith as an action. Or it could be said that as the heart-soul honors the truth of Lord Jesus, the will-soul bends and welcomes the truth of the spirit body to reign in the soul body. A shifting within the heart-soul of loyalty and beliefs overrides what has been before. Thus, a war within the believer happens as the spirit is welcomed to communicate with the soul and to overcome the past dependency on the fleshly body. This is why the verse in Galatians is so important as a declaration of faith and intent. As stated in Galatians 2:20:

> *I have been crucified with Christ; it is no longer I who live, but Christ lives in me; and the life which I now live in the flesh I live by faith in the Son of God, who loved me and gave Himself for me.*

A decision to kill the old heart-soul happens when Jesus is declared Lord and given authority over the soul. A surrender of the will-soul to the truths of the spirit over the flesh-based knowing is included in the crucifixion of the soul body. Welcoming Christ to live and function is one's spirit body and soul body is a choice. Living by faith is the action of trusting the new life in the spirit over the old way of knowing. Notice the faith is dependent on acknowledging the love of God. The seeker has moved back into righteous relationship through the faith actions grounded in love. God's provision through His grace of the gift of salvation for those who believe invites the seeker to return God's love. Now it is more than loyalty to God that drives a person's choice. Living by faith implies returning love to God for all He provides. Love for God is the substance that supports faith actions.

Think and write about it

1. Describe the difference between the Kingdom of God and heaven.

2. When were you enlisted in the war between God and His enemy?

3. What is your assignment as a member of the army of God?

\
4. How do faith and love relate?

Summary

In these first two verses of the Lord's Prayer, there are five basic concepts the seeker discovers to form a more intimate relationship with God and submit to God's plans and ways. King Jesus is the way, the truth, and the example to follow. In applying these concepts, an intimate relationship with God develops. The seeker learns the heart of God and the will of God. When the seeker approaches God as a child, a proper learning relationship occurs. The goal is total dependency on God. It is fulfilling the first and the greatest commandment to love God with one's whole heart, whole soul, and whole mind (Mathew 22:37 & Luke 10:27)

Five Concepts:

1. Surrender of personal will and power to God is essential.

2. Praise and honor God daily for who He is.

3. Seek God with your whole heart-soul.

4. Know the rules governing the Kingdom of God and align with the Kingdom of God

5. As a member of the army of God, follow the directives of the Commander, King Jesus.

6

King David's Tabernacle

Those in covenant with God choose to honor His ways and bring His will into this earthly realm. We become the body of Christ in this earth. As mature believers, the body is to come together to do the work of the Kingdom of God on this earth. This is our responsibility as members of the blood covenant we hold with God. God has commanded times and places where this is to occur. Not only in obedience, but also in love for our God do members of the body seek to unite. As mature sons and daughters of God we come to worship and honor our God. As noted in earlier chapters, love is active and focused on the beloved. Love comes from God and in worship we return it to God. As stated in Hebrews 13:15:

Therefore, by Him let us continually offer the sacrifice of praise to God, that is, the fruit of our lips, giving thanks to His name.

In gratitude and love we give honor to God for the life, death, and resurrection of King Jesus. We also give thanks and praise for the living King Jesus who lives in us. In unity as the body of Christ, our praise opens doors to heaven. Now as the head and body are united, the work of the government of God can be enacted within the earthly realm.

Believers have individual opportunities for daily worship. Daily entering prayer closets to communicate with God is a form of worship. Worship can be carried throughout the day through speaking in tongues and praising God with God honoring music. When a person meditates on a scripture throughout the day, that is also worship. Romans 12:1 states:

I beseech you therefore, brethren, by the mercies of God, that you present your bodies a living sacrifice, holy, acceptable to God, which is your reasonable service.

Paul is explaining the daily submission of all three bodies in service to God. Each of us does this individually as led by the Holy Spirit. In worship, we serve our God both individually and corporately.

Besides individual responsibilities within covenant, we share a corporate responsibility. Jesus prayed for this as recorded in John 17:23

I in them, and You in Me; that they may be made perfect in one, and that the world may know that You have sent Me, and have loved them as You have loved Me.

Jesus is calling His believers to be united as one. Paul describes how all become one body in 1 Corinthians 12:12 -31. Each member contributes to the whole with the spiritual gifts God has granted individuals. To operate in this God-planned manner, each person is to submit their gifts under the direction of the Holy Spirit. When functioning in unity, Paul states in 1 Corinthians 12:25 – 26:

> *...25that there should be no schism in the body, but that the members should have the same care for one another. 26And if one member suffers, all the members suffer with it; or if one member is honored, all the members rejoice with it.*

As described in earlier chapters, the goal of this type of unity is reached in surrender to God and love for God. Believers' number one focus is on God, not the body of Christ or self. Our commission is to bring the active love of God into a world that does not honor or recognize our God for who He is (John 17:23). We are to demonstrate the love of God. God left signposts in our world to indicate His Kingdom Principles. One of these signposts is numbers. Multiple truths are found in each number. The mutual supportive love of Father God, Jesus Christ and Holy Spirit is embodied in the number three. God's repeated use of the number three may remind us that the God-ordained pattern of how love is to be brought into our world. Here is one application of that pattern:

> ➢ *God first loves us* and sends Jesus Christ to reconcile us to God by grace. When we accept the gift of love by grace, we join into this love. We honor that love by returning it to God as we submit to his authority in our lives. We join with God in love, cleansing ourselves to prepare a holy place for God to reside.

> ➢ *We seek other believers* with whom to unite to serve God's will and plans for this earth. We become Kingdom of God builders in our earth as it is in heaven. We honor our part of covenant by becoming the family of God, sharing love with each other.

> ➢ *We take this love into the world*, spreading the Gospel of God's truth to those still caught in darkness. We complete the assignment given to Noah, Abraham, Moses, and Jesus Christ to possess and occupy the land for our God.

God's plans empower a group of people who love God above all else and share that love in unity to bring it into a lost world that is blinded by the enemy. People are caught in the enemy's traps and darkness (Ephesians 4:18 - 19). Many do not even know they are slaves to this system. Through the darkening of their soul-hearts, many cannot see the soul chains within the world system. These prisoners of darkness are so blind they do not even know they agreed to the lies that trapped them in the enemy's system. The type of unified body Christ Jesus prayed His people to be is not known in the world's system (John 17:16). Staying in the covenant with

God by faith demonstrates to people trapped in darkness that God loves us. The power of love to heal, reconcile, and bring blessings during the attacks from the enemy in our lives becomes apparent to those caught in darkness. Our witness and manner of relating to each other demonstrates who God is and what he has done for us. God's love overcomes through the body of Christ. As we take our place as ambassadors for God's Kingdom on earth, we rule and bring order back to our earthly realm.

Think and write about it

1. What are the individual responsibilities of a believer under the covenant of the blood of Jesus?

2. What are the corporate responsibilities of believers under the blood covenant of Jesus?

3. What is the purpose of corporate gatherings of believers in Jesus Christ as Lord?

Unity as one body in Christ is imperative to accomplish this task. It was recorded in Acts 2; the first believers to join the apostles were functioning this way (Acts 2:44). It is noted what they did together in Acts 2:46 – 47:

> *⁴⁶So continuing daily with one accord in the temple, and breaking bread from house to house, they ate their food with gladness and simplicity of heart,*

> *⁴⁷praising God and having favor with all the people. And the Lord added to the church daily those who were being saved.*

There is a protocol for functioning as the living body of Christ. These believers met in the temple daily. It was their joy to go and give praise and honor to God. This type of devotion is also recorded in 1 Chronicles 16. King David appointed people to serve in the temple 24 hours each day. They not only observed the sacrifices according to the directions from Moses, but they also had music and praise throughout the day. When Solomon completed the new temple, he again instituted the same pattern of worship in addition to all the requirements Moses recorded from God (2 Chronicles 8:14 – 15). This method of worship is known as Davidic Worship. In other instances in the Bible, praise is recognized as an essential element to enter God's presence. Psalm 22:3 states God inhabits the praises of His people. The first protocol for living in unity as the body of Christ is meeting regularly. The second is to honor God in praise. Praise released from the heart-souls of those who have the spirit of Jesus abiding in them invites God into their presence. It is an act of faith and love combined. The body of Christ is united to the head which is Jesus Christ through this active praise and worship.

As recognized in an earlier chapter, the purpose of meeting regularly is to accomplish the work of the body of Christ in this earth. We are to align with God's Kingdom and enforce it in our territories. Psalm 24 gives a pattern to accomplish this alignment and unity with our head, Jesus Christ. King David wrote this psalm as a prophetic pattern for those who wanted to worship as he did. All true worship begins with acknowledging who God is. Just as Jesus did when he gave the Lord's prayer, the first thing to do when seeking God in unity is to acknowledge God. The first two verses recognize the fundamental truth of who God is. Psalm 24: 1 -2:

> *The earth is the LORD's, and all its fullness, The world and those who dwell therein.*
> *² For He has founded it upon the seas, And established it upon the waters.*

The attribute that God is Creator and sustainer of all is the foundation of building a relationship with God. True Davidic worship is relational. The created person seeks God. Believers who acknowledge Jesus Christ as the Son of God desire to know more about the amazing gift of grace and the love of God for His creation. The wisdom a person has gained through the Bible drives a person to know God in greater depths. Gratitude leads the heart to worship.

A need develops in the worshipper to seek greater unity with our God. Psalm 24 states the question behind this need. As recorded in Psalm 24:3

> *³ Who may ascend into the hill of the LORD? Or who may stand in His holy place?*

The love for God and the love received from God cause believers to seek unity. In the spirit realm, like seeks like. There is a need for completion. In the completion, the love multiplies and explodes. Spirit meets spirit. So, in honoring God, the seeker now wants to know who can enter into greater unity with this love. Psalm 24:4 gives the answer.

> *⁴ He who has clean hands and a pure heart, Who has not lifted up his soul to an idol, Nor sworn deceitfully.*

Who may ascend into the Glory of the Lord God? Only someone:

> ➤ With clean hands and pure heart
>
> ➤ Whose soul is not lifted in pride and filled with guile.
>
> ➤ Who does not attempt to deceive God.
>
> ➤ Who does not place worldly desires above the love for God.

Clean hands are hands of innocent or blameless people. Those who have accepted Jesus Christ as Redeemer and Savior, declaring with their mouths this belief in their hearts, have received salvation. These are the ones whose hands are clean. In Father God's eyes, when He looks at them, He sees Jesus. A pure soul-heart is one that has been emptied of anything that does not honor God. Believers in Jesus Christ who have placed themselves under the lordship of Jesus and followed the requirements of sanctification have emptied their soul-hearts of anything that is not honoring to God. People who declare Jesus Christ is the only Son of God and Lord of all creation, develop a personal relationship with God through daily prayer, Bible reading and mediation, daily praise, and daily praying in tongues. Over time, they no longer operate in the guile of the world's systems or lift themselves up in pride (1 John 3:9). Their confidence is in Jesus Christ alone and who they are in Jesus Christ. These people no longer have double mindedness in their soul-hearts. Their loyalty is first and foremost to God above all. They have a personal relationship with the Holy Spirit through the baptism of the Holy Spirit (1 John 2:27). The believers at this level regularly speak in tongues or in their prayer language. These followers of Jesus Christ who have this relationship with the Holy Spirit rely on the Holy Spirit to convict them of anything against God. When convicted they immediately move into confession and repentance of whatever has created barriers with God (1 John 1:9). The results of these actions are that the person has balanced one's heart, mind, and will to function as a unit in the spiritual realm. These are the people God invites to rise within the glory of God and enter deeper into His spiritual temple.

When we corporately seek to enter the presence of God through the glory of God, together we are to surrender to God's authority. It is done each time the body of Christ gathers. It is, in essence, knocking on the door that is King Jesus. Psalm 24:5 - 6 describes this:

⁵ He shall receive blessing from the LORD, And righteousness from the God of his salvation. ⁶ This is Jacob, the generation of those who seek Him, Who seek Your face.

Verse 5 declares the promise to those who turn their lives over to Jesus Christ as Lord and master. We are to be blessed. As stated in 2 Corinthians 5:21:

For He made Him who knew no sin to be sin for us, that we might become the righteousness of God in Him.

Salvation comes through Jesus Christ alone. He is the door. It is done in faith. No individual effort or works can accomplish earning salvation. Surrender is the key. Turning one's will over to the truth of who Jesus Christ is and walking in faith is how salvation is accomplished. In Davidic Worship, the worshipper declares these truths. Together, in faith and in worship, the people submit their personal wills to God. This permits them to move in unity into a deeper relationship with God. Honor is given to God for accomplishing salvation through the blood of Jesus Christ. Our relationship as created and reborn children of Creator God is declared. This surrender and declaration meet Kingdom of God protocol for entering the courts of heaven to do Kingdom business.

Verse six refers to the desire to seek God's face. Jacob did this when he wrestled with God (Genesis 32:24 – 30). He did this alone, at night. Jacob sought God and His blessing. In the protocol for actively participating in Davidic worship, David is explaining what is done individually before entering corporate worship. Believers who seek God's face in corporate worship have first sought Him privately. They have wrestled with God, giving up what was not of God and binding the blessings of God to their soul bodies. Knowing this union with God, they now combine with other like-minded believers to seek God's face.

Seeking the face of God is more than accomplishing the list of activities and change of soul-mind and soul-heart. Abraham walked with God and knew Him. Moses sought the face of God. David sought this type of relationship when he sought God with his whole heart. For these three mentioned, it is a journey directed by the Holy Spirit. Like any journey there are challenges. To continue the journey requires determination and courage. There is a cost greater than what has already been paid in the process described above. The rest of this psalm explains the process of seeking the face of God. The desire to be in greater union with God can be achieved in corporate Davidic worship. It is through entering the manifest glory of God.

Now two basic steps for entering into corporate Davidic worship are completed. *The first is claiming who God is by recognizing some of His attributes. The second is again acknowledging who King Jesus Christ is and who we are in Jesus.* Both are active corporate surrender of one's will to Father God, His Son King Jesus, and the teacher of truth, Holy Spirit. *A third step in Davidic worship is completed individually before entering the sanctuary of God.* The question in verse 3 and the answer are the patterns of an individual building a relationship with God. *To rise up in another level of relationship and Davidic worship requires this time spent outside of corporate worship.*

Verse seven states to lift up our heads. As noted, Psalm 24:7:

> *⁷Lift up your heads, O you gates! And be lifted up, you everlasting doors! And the King of glory shall come in.*

Figuratively, this is the physical head. Spiritually, it is focusing on what is above us, our Lord, the resurrected King Jesus. To corporately enter this journey of seeking the face of God, believers are to focus on God. Look up to the destination one is seeking! Eyes are the windows to the soul (Matthew 6: 22 – 24). Even though people have surrendered themselves to God in the previous actions, thoughts, and emotions listed in verse four, now is a time of deeper surrender. Jesus stated once our hand is on the plow not to look back (Luke 9:62). He told His disciples those who had to care for the worldly needs first were not fit to be disciples (Luke 9: 59 – 61). This is not a harsh statement. Jesus is speaking the truth that the motivation behind the seeking is the central desire of the people at this time. It is the will of the people that have chosen to enter deeper in worship to seek the face of God. No other desire from the world can now overtake believers in this time as they seek God.

Verse seven also mentions gates. Modern western thinking does not grasp what these gates are. **Strong's H8179** provides the translation for *gates* in this passage. It is an opening, or passageway. The entrance or opening on this spiritual journey is through the spirit and soul. As noted earlier, the eyes are the windows of the soul. Scripture also states the hearing of the word of God opens the soul to know and understand the perfect will of God (Romans 10:17). The spiritual journey into a greater relationship with God is through opening of the soul-mind into one's spirit body. It is accomplished through the aid of the Holy Spirit. Since the soul and spirit are the eternal aspects of a person, the psalm calls these gates, everlasting doors. The goal is a closer relationship with almighty God. Jesus is the door and the way into a greater relationship with Father God. The goal described in this part of the psalm is to ascend into the throne room of God through His manifested glory. To see and hear in this realm, active and conscious spiritual eyes and ears are required. Corporately, people are to focus their soul-minds on God and open their consciousness within their spirit bodies.

The purpose of entering the courts of heaven is twofold. We, His people, unite to be the body of Christ. Our first purpose is to give thanksgiving and glory to our creator. It is an act of love, not obligation. As John stated, God first loved us and created us out of love (1 John 4:16 – 19). When we are fully awake in the spirit, we know who we are. *Agape* love grows in the uncluttered soul. A desire for greater union with the creator grows. Thus, the next verse in psalm 24 grows within the spirit/soul of the believer. Psalm 24:8

> *Who is this King of glory? The LORD strong and mighty, The LORD mighty in battle.*

When a seeker uses one's spiritual language in the glory, spiritual eyes and ears are opened wider. In corporate unity believers have bound their wills to the Holy Spirit in surrender. There is an urgency in the spirit to move up higher into spiritual realms. Letting go of one's own orientation in the physical world and allowing the truth of the spiritual realm to be the focus of the combined wills of self and the Holy Spirit open spiritual ears and eyes further. Now the united corporate body senses deeper movement in the glory. Believers who have accepted Jesus as Lord knows we have access through grace to this experience in the glory. We acknowledge it is God who battled by the blood of Jesus to free us from the power of the law of sin and death. By the righteousness of Jesus Christ bonded to our souls, we have the right to enter the glory as co-heirs with our God. This is accomplished in more worship and declaration by the people.

The psalm repeats and adds the final approach within the glory for the corporate body of Jesus Christ to accomplish. Psalm 24: 9

> *Lift up your heads, O you gates! Lift up, you everlasting doors! And the King of glory shall come in.*

In the presence of our almighty King, we have a responsibility to complete Kingdom business. This is the united subjects, have the second part of the twofold purpose of meeting corporately. We have invited our King into our presence, and we have sought Him in heaven. Now we listen to His commands and enact them. Words of wisdom swirl in this glory. Scripture is alive and moving in the glory. As seekers sense these things, the worshippers are to call them out. Declaring brings into the physical realm what is not already there from what is in the spiritual realm. These are spiritual truths and attributes of our triune God. We sense them for we are familiar with them. They have been written on our souls. In the glory, like attracts like. God is bringing His presence and gifts from the third heaven into this world. As stated in Matthew 16:19, King Jesus has given believers authority to release what is in heaven. If worshippers fail to speak these things out, they will remain in the third heaven. Believers are to speak out what is being offered to aid God's people.

The light of God will then shine on the ways His people are moving. King Jesus is the light incarnate. In the light all darkness is overcome. The life of God is in the light

As believers achieved this level of involvement with God and His glory, they can now ask God as intercessors for others. He will listen to our prayers and consider our requests for others. God also knows the hearts of all people. Burdens people are carrying into the glory are exposed for God to cleanse and heal as the people join in worshipping God. Some of what is called from the glory is hope, healing waters, love from God, grace of God for those who are trapped in depression and other bondages. These are anointings being released. Again, believers are to speak them out to demonstrate acceptance and acknowledgement of them. Once recognized or released, these anointings then are carried by angels to people participating in the glory. The corporate body may also intercede for regions or nations. Again, what is sensed in the glory is released through declarations. All of this is completing Kingdom business. We are to possess and occupy the spiritual land. His body is to declare God's truth and call alignment with Kingdom of God principles in our earth as it is in heaven.

The final act of Davidic worship is to acknowledge and give honor to our source of life and healing, King Jesus. As stated in verse 10:

> ¹⁰ *Who is this King of glory? The* LORD *of hosts, He is the King of glory.*

Who is the King of glory the psalm asks? The Lord King Jesus who is strong in battle. As the corporate body has brought forth what God wanted to release from the spirit realm into the earthly realm, a battle was fought, and victory belongs to King Jesus. The cycle in the glory is not complete until honor is given to the divine door, King Jesus. All that has been released now is returned to our eternal source. Glory is given as gratitude wells up in the spirits and souls of the worshippers. At this level of involvement with the glory, it is paramount all glory is returned to our King Jesus. As stated in John 16:14, the acts of the Holy Spirit will glorify Jesus. This worship into the glory was led by the Holy Spirit. Now acknowledgement and honor are returned to our Lord and King Jesus. As stated in John 16:15,

> *All things that the Father has are Mine. Therefore I said that He will take of Mine and declare it to you.*

We give thanks for working together with our King to complete Kingdom of God business in unity with our God and one another.

Think and write about it

1. *What is the protocol for functioning in the living Body of Christ?*

2. *What steps in Davidic worship are necessary for entering the presence of God?*

3. *How do believers know their soul-hearts have no guile?*

4. *Describe how a person seeks God's face in their prayer closet.*

5. *Describe the work of God's Kingdom done through corporate worship.*

7

Principles of the Kingdom of God

Life is maintained in our earthly realm when we are aligned with the principles of God's Kingdom. God has made these principles known to His people through His word recorded in the Bible, with His words given in revelation through His prophets, and through intimate, direct interaction with our triune God. Jesus Christ, the Word of God, came in the flesh to demonstrate how to operate in tandem with Kingdom of God principles while living in a fleshly body (John 1:14). As noted in earlier chapters, God created humanity to be His family to live with Him. We were created in their (Father, Son and Holy Spirit) likeness with free will to choose to be part of this family. The choice is to submit to the order and harmony in creation or to rebel against it. Again, choosing to rebel is choosing to empower chaos and leads to death. Choosing life is choosing to be in covenant with God and to live within the rules and regulations that keep balance within the living entity of God's Kingdom.

God's enemy actively works to destroy covenant and subvert humanity to serve him. As noted earlier, those who choose to honor God and make Jesus Christ their Lord, have entered into this battle. The body of Christ is to know the principles of God's Kingdom and to apply them to complete our covenantal agreement with God. We are to war on God's terms, not the enemy's. Jesus Christ has already defeated the enemy. We are simply to enforce that victory. In unity with our Lord, King Jesus, with the aid of the Holy Spirit, we follow God's battle plan to bring his Kingdom into our earthly realm just as we pray in the Lord's Prayer. We are to take the word of God, in all of the ways God gives it to us, to use as a weapon against our common enemy. As it is stated in Hebrews 4:12

> *For the word of God is living and powerful, and sharper than any two-edged sword, piercing even to the division of soul and spirit, and of joints and marrow, and is a discerner of the thoughts and intents of the heart.*

For our common enemy is spiritual. The enemy, a created being who was removed from heaven by God's will, still must function within the system of government God created to accomplish His desires (Isaiah 14: 12 – 15). As one who is created, only the created system can be accessed. He lacks the ability to create anything different. The enemy's plans include focusing our understanding on the physical level. At this level the enemy hopes to distract us from these powerful weapons of the words of God and the truth that Jesus Christ has already won the victory. If we are ignorant of the spiritual tools and weapons we have, we remain trapped in a soul mindset focused on the physical realm. As stated in Ephesians 6:12

> *For we do not wrestle against flesh and blood, but against principalities, against powers, against the rulers of the darkness of this age, against spiritual hosts of wickedness in the heavenly places.*

We are to battle in the spirit, for spiritual territory, to free the earthly realm from the influence of our common enemy. This means operating within the divine order of creation and maintaining it on earth as it is in heaven. As stated in 2 Corinthians 2:11:

> *…lest Satan should take advantage of us; for we are not ignorant of his devices.*

As we learn how to live in both the earthly realm and the spiritual realm while in our physical bodies, we take possession of the victory Jesus Christ has already won for us. The battle is God's, and we apply His battle plan to cleanse the earth through our spirits, alive in King Jesus.

Think and Write about it

1. How does submission to God and His covenant maintain life on earth?

2. What is one of the plans of the enemy?

We know our Creator God planned for all things to return to proper alignment in His governmental system. Before He began re-creating earth from the formless darkness and the deep, a plan for redemption was established but hidden in His mysteries (Ephesians 1: 9 - 11). The coming of Jesus Christ as the perfect lamb, sacrificed for the redemption of the world, was planned by our triune God. As recorded in 1 Peter 1:20 – 21:

20He indeed was foreordained before the foundation of the world but was manifest in these last times for you 21who through Him believe in God, who raised Him from the dead and gave Him glory, so that your faith and hope are in God.

Destroying the power and influence of God's enemy over humanity was determined by God before creation. We who accept this returning to right relationship in covenant with God enter into this promise through faith. We engage in this battle. We know truth and truth sets us free (John 8:32). In Creator God's magnificent plans, He ordained a way for the new covenant to be written on our soul-hearts and minds. As recorded in Hebrews 8: 10 – 12

10"For this is the covenant that I will make with the house of Israel after those days, says the LORD: I will put My laws in their mind and write them on their hearts; and I will be their God, and they shall be My people. 11"None of them shall teach his neighbor, and none his brother, saying, 'Know the LORD,' for all shall know Me, from the least of them to the greatest of them. 12"For I will be merciful to their unrighteousness, and their sins and their lawless deeds I will remember no more."

As mature believers in Jesus Christ as our Lord, we rise in our spirit bodies and apply the principles of God's Kingdom while living in this earthly realm.

Some of the Principles of the Kingdom of God were alluded to in previous chapters. These will be reviewed and expanded in this chapter. Foremost is how we, God's people who have accepted the grace of God to become His people, are to relate to our God. As mentioned in the first chapter, it began with Adam. God's grace and love are the avenues to begin a relationship with God. It is accessed through faith, not works or dependency on the physical realm. It is the first principle of the Kingdom of God. The blending of God's love for His creation and His calling of people (which is Grace) is an active, living entity in the Kingdom of God. Recognizing this pull from the spiritual realm is the first step in aligning with Kingdom of God principles. Responding in faith is how one connects with this grace and love. God offers us, while we are still not in proper relationship with Him, His grace and mercy to enter the blood covenant with Jesus Christ (Romans 5:8). Grace is the result of active seeking of God for human hearts that turn from this worldview to Him. God's love creates moments in our lives for us to choose to accept Him and His love. Faith and trust in what are not seen in the physical realm is our response. Our free-will response of trust and faith to God's ways is like a baby's first step. The pattern is learned to hear God's calling and to follow with surrender of one's will to God's purpose. The rhythm of God's grace and love reaching a person and then the person surrendering one's will in love and obedience is beginning to form. It is cyclical and living in the spiritual realm. This is the first principle of God's Kingdom.

The second principle is like the first. God knows as learners we will make mistakes and have missteps. He also knows the enemy will set traps full of lies and illusions to pull us off our journey with God. When we fall into these traps, regret and other forms of sorrow can lead to our choosing to separate ourselves from God. As Paul explains, there is a method to return to God. He recorded it is 2 Corinthians 7:10:

> *For godly sorrow produces repentance leading to salvation, not to be regretted; but the sorrow of the world produces death.*

A system of returning to proper alignment with God's Kingdom principles was created. It is the second principle of the Kingdom of God. It consists of:

- ➢ Seek God to admit participating in actions, thoughts, or beliefs outside of covenant with Him.

- ➢ Confess and accept ownership of being in rebellion

- ➢ Lay it on the cross of Jesus

- ➢ Exchange the earned harvest of separation from God's covenant for the blood of Jesus Christ in our place. This is accepting God's Grace.

- ➢ Receive forgiveness from God thus returning to right relationship with God.

- ➢ Seek God and His kingdom to rule in our lives again.

Forgiveness is this Kingdom Principle for returning to right relationship with God. God expects His people to walk in faith, not their own works. He knows we are learners. He does not expect perfectionism in this walk. At one point God tells His people they are clay pots He has molded to serve His purposes (Jeremiah 18:1 – 6). Paul expands this concept to let us know it is not our own strength that brings victory, as noted in 2 Corinthians 4:7 – 9:

> *⁷But we have this treasure in earthen vessels, that the excellence of the power may be of God and not of us. ⁸We are hard-pressed on every side, yet not crushed; we are perplexed, but not in despair; ⁹persecuted, but not forsaken; struck down, but not destroyed...*

Through ever attack of the enemy, we have this principle of forgiveness. If we fall and lose our direction, it is God who will bring us back under covenant with the principle of forgiveness. Like the first Kingdom of God principle, this is an interaction with God. Forgiveness is alive and an attribute of God. Like all principles, it is an intimate part of our relationship with God.

King David wrote about the nature of God's forgiveness in Psalm 103:8 – 10 (NIV):

⁸The LORD is compassionate and gracious, slow to anger, abounding in love. ⁹He will not always accuse, nor will he harbor his anger forever; ¹⁰he does not treat us as our sins deserve or repay us according to our iniquities.

When we acknowledge our actions and choices have separated us from God, we enter into God's grace as David describes. By the blood of Jesus, we are not treated as our sins deserve. David notes the extent of God's forgiveness in verse 12 (NIV):

…as far as the east is from the west, so far has he removed our transgressions from us.

God's nature is such that what has been forgiven is removed from any memory or record kept in heaven. The enemy of God may try to bring back events and create guilt for what has been forgiven. He wants us to re-own and bury guilt in our soul-hearts. God has erased the transgression by the blood of Jesus. In the acts of forgiveness, we return to covenant with God. God's heart for the Kingdom Principle of forgiveness is summarized in verses 17 – 18 of Psalm 103 (NIV).

¹⁷But from everlasting to everlasting the LORD's love is with those who fear him, and his righteousness with their children's children— ¹⁸with those who keep his covenant and remember to obey his precepts.

Forgiveness is a method for God's people to remain in covenant with Him. By participating in forgiveness, God's people function within a shared love relationship.

This Kingdom of God principle of forgiveness encompasses how we relate to others as well as how we relate to God. This principle has two sides to it. One involves forgiveness concerning ourselves and God and the other side between other people and us. In earlier chapters the Lord's Prayer was used as a model for seeking God. Another verse in the Lord's prayer, recorded in Luke 11:4 states:

And forgive us our sins, For we also forgive everyone who is indebted to us.

Jesus is teaching the full principle of the Kingdom of God, which is a living forgiveness. The body of Christ is a corporate body, in unity with God and each other. Jesus commanded His disciples to love one another as He loved them (John 14:34). People carry seeds of iniquity when they withhold forgiveness from someone else. These seeds can become roots of bitterness if not destroyed immediately. A person who harbors a root of bitterness is double minded. As Jesus stated in Matthew 6:14 – 15

¹⁴For if you forgive men their trespasses, your heavenly Father will also forgive you. ¹⁵But if you do not forgive men their trespasses, neither will your Father forgive your trespasses.

One's unforgiveness limits what God can do in a person's life. God is blocked by this barrier a person created. It builds strongholds in the soul body. This stronghold honors self, feeding rebellion. It prevents a person from growing closer to God. Surrendering of one's own will to live in God's will destroys this stronghold. The action needed is forgiveness of the other person. It has nothing to do with offense and who is right, and everything to do with staying in covenant with God. People who are surrendered to the will of God place God's priority over their own.

As noted in an earlier chapter, brotherly love is required to enter the presence of God in corporate worship to complete the business of the Kingdom of God. The fullness of this Kingdom of God principle of forgiveness creates peace and unity with others as well as with God. Jesus explained this in Matthew 5:23 - 24

> 23*"Therefore if you bring your gift to the altar, and there remember that your brother has something against you, 24leave your gift there before the altar, and go your way. First be reconciled to your brother, and then come and offer your gift.*

Gifts were given for multiple reasons. Many times, these gifts were thanksgiving offerings for actions God completed in a person's life. Jesus turns the cultural understanding around in this statement. He makes it clear that being in righteous relationship with others is a requirement before giving gratitude to God. The bitter root buried in the soul body caught in unforgiveness of the one offering a gift, has a stronghold on the person. By seeking reconciliation with the other person, the stronghold is broken. Being at peace with others in the body of Christ is essential to being in right relationship with God. Now the offering is given from a purified heart-soul. It is pleasing to God when given from this type of heart-soul.

Jesus further develops this concept of forgiveness in Matthew chapter five. Another reason for presenting gifts to God is to atone for actions committed by individuals that broke covenant with God. Verses 25 through 26 describe the reason for the need of atonement. Jewish people understood these verses reflected a spiritual truth. Our action can give the enemy of God the legal right to enter a person's life. As recorded in verse 25 - 26

> *"Agree with your adversary quickly, while you are on the way with him, lest your adversary deliver you to the judge, the judge hand you over to the officer, and you be thrown into prison.* 26*Assuredly, I say to you, you will by no means get out of there till you have paid the last penny.*

Jesus is speaking about the courts of heaven. The adversary is God's enemy. Committing an offense against the law of God gives the enemy of God the legal right to gain a legal judgment against the person who has broken the laws of God. It builds iniquity in the life of the individual. Breaking the law places a person outside of covenant with God. God's protection is achieved only in covenant. The legal right allows the enemy to hold the person in spiritual bondage. With blood sacrifices, like those recorded in Leviticus, atonement for transgressions against God was paid.

After completing atonement, a person returned to right relationship with God. Now Jesus is raising the level of the transgression of unforgiveness to destroying covenant with God. Though not specifically mentioned in the Levitical laws, unforgiveness is an extension of the ten commandments. Jesus is telling us to admit the transgression quickly. Confess the unforgiveness immediately! We who are under the blood covenant of Jesus owe our righteous standing with God to His blood (2 Corinthians 5:21). Move quickly into admitting any transgression and then ask for our advocate, King Jesus, to cover us in the heavenly court. In court, we admit the transgression, but also point out our righteousness is in Jesus our Lord. We enact both sides of forgiveness. First with God, then with people. This is how the principle of forgiveness functions in both relationship with God and our fellow humans.

For modern believers in Jesus Christ as Lord, this concept of heavenly courts tends to be overlooked. It is imperative that we embrace the truth of how the courts function as we learn Kingdom of God principles. The first principle of the Kingdom of God granted a legal right to those who confess Jesus Christ as Lord. It is recorded in the Book of Life, a legal document in heaven's courts. God's Kingdom is a kingdom of order and harmony. Besides knowing the Kingdom of God principles, we are to understand the protocol for entering the courts of heaven. An earlier chapter explained this protocol. We, His ambassadors on earth, are to honor our King and function in His authority and power. Our God dispenses His judgments for His people in these courts. Jesus Christ is our advocate (1 John 2:1). The enemy of God is our accuser (Revelation 12:10). The Holy Spirit is our witness (Acts 5:32). Jesus Christ gave us the right to enter the court while still in our physical bodies to demand justice against a lawless enemy that will not respect our God. As noted in Hebrews 4:16:

> *Let us therefore come boldly to the throne of grace, that we may obtain mercy and find grace to help in time of need.*

As noted earlier, when the body of Christ comes together, one of its functions is to complete the business of the Kingdom of God. God's word is a sword we may use to enforce King Jesus' victory. The enemy of God, who was completely defeated by King Jesus, still roams this earth (Job 17:8 & 1 Peter 5:8). Jesus Christ instructed us so we would be aware of the enemy's tactics. When we stand in faith in the victory of King Jesus, we have the tools to subdue our common enemy. The adversary cannot win judgements against the people of God when we know how to function in this heavenly court. Operating within the total principle of forgiveness provides believers with one tool to defeat the enemy. Staying in right relationship with God allows us to enter the heavenly courts and demand justice. This is one of the blessings of being under the covenant of the blood of Jesus Christ.

The courts of heaven also hear petitions from the people of God. When we pray for God to intercede in our lives, we are petitioning the courts of heaven. John records this in one of his letters. As stated in 1 John 5:14 – 15

14Now this is the confidence that we have in Him, that if we ask anything according to His will, He hears us. 15And if we know that He hears us, whatever we ask, we know that we have the petitions that we have asked of Him.

Entering in the spiritual realm with an awakened spirit body is achieved when we align with God's will. We trust God's promises when we rest in His will. As stated in the previous chapters, it is in faith we enter the spiritual realm where the courts of heaven are located. Jesus Christ gave the protocol in the Lord's prayer for petitioning God. In faith we begin by declaring who God is. We honor and recognize His power and authority in our lives. This sets our soul-hearts and soul-minds in submission under God's will. It is an act of faith each time a petitioner seeks access to God's courts of heaven. As stated in Ephesians 6: 17 – 18

17And take the helmet of salvation, and the sword of the Spirit, which is the word of God; 18praying always with all prayer and supplication in the Spirit, being watchful to this end with all perseverance and supplication for all the saints…

We live under the authority of salvation in Jesus Christ. This helmet governs our thinking. We yield to our spirit-mind. The words of God recorded in the Bible along with prophetic words given by the Holy Spirit form the sword of the spirit. Aligning with these words as well as declaring them out loud brings them into the court room of heaven. It is under the authority of King Jesus, in unity with other believers, we submit to the will of God. As Jesus stated in Mathew 18:19 – 20

19"Again I say to you that if two of you agree on earth concerning anything that they ask, it will be done for them by My Father in heaven. 20For where two or three are gathered together in My name, I am there in the midst of them."

As the Lord's Prayer states, we petition for the will of God to be made known in our earthly realm. We walk in the faith of Abraham (Romans 4:17). We call that which is not present in our earthly realm to be made manifest now from the heavenly realm. Agreeing with God's will and functioning within the Kingdom of God principles allows us to bring the Kingdom of God on earth as it is in heaven.

Think and Write about it

1. Describe the first principle of the Kingdom of God.

2. Describe the second principle of the Kingdom of God.

3. What are the courts of heaven and how do they operate?

The third principle in God's Kingdom establishes His judgment and righteousness. As noted earlier, God's love, grace, and mercy formed creation. His justice and righteousness align creation with the harmonies in the heavenly Kingdom. As noted by David in two psalms:

Psalm 111:3

His work is honorable and glorious, And His righteousness endures forever.

Psalm 119:137 - 138

Righteous are You, O LORD, And upright are Your judgments. [138]*Your testimonies, which You have commanded, Are righteous and very faithful.*

Righteousness holds everything in proper alignment. Balance and order, to the original intent of God, is preserved through this third principle. The Kingdom of God principle is the system of seedtime, growth time and harvest time. As noted in earlier chapters, God taught Adam this principle when He required him to tend the garden. Father God also taught Noah this principle after the ark landed (Genesis 8:22). Again, He taught Moses the same principle. It is embedded in scripture for all who seek God to find Him. Jesus Christ taught it in His parables. The parable of the sower is recorded in Matthew 13: 1 – 23, Mark 4: 13– 20, and Luke 8: 11– 15. By our actions and our words, we participate in the principle of seedtime, growth time and harvest time. It is automatic, not a choice. Whether or not we agree with the system does not matter. It exists by divine planning and execution. As Jesus stated, what we say with our mouths is the result of what we harbor in our soul-hearts (Luke 6:46). We either agree in submission to God or we rebel. Obedience leads to words and actions that honor God and rebellion leads to actions and words that curse God.

As noted in earlier chapters, what we say with our mouths has spiritual consequences. By the use of our tongue, we choose life or death. As recorded in Proverbs 18:21

> *Death and life are in the power of the tongue, And those who love it will eat its fruit.*

Whatever is planted in words is grown over time and produces fruit in the spiritual realm. Two places record these events. One is in our soul bodies. The other is stored in our book of remembrance in heaven (Malachi 3:16). We commit to our soul-heart choices when we release words. Proverbs 16:27 – 28 explains this.

> *27An ungodly man digs up evil, And it is on his lips like a burning fire. 28A perverse man sows strife, And a whisperer separates the best of friends.*

We choose rebellion when we create strife. It is usually for our own gain. On the other hand, Proverbs 16: 23 – 24 states:

> *23The heart of the wise teaches his mouth, And adds learning to his lips. 24Pleasant words are like a honeycomb, Sweetness to the soul and health to the bones.*

The soul-heart which has bound God's words to it has taught itself wisdom. These words produce life in a person's soul and physical body. Jesus warned the people in Matthew 12:36 – 37 of the consequences for what we say.

> *36"But I say to you that for every idle word men may speak, they will give account of it in the day of judgment. 37For by your words you will be justified, and by your words you will be condemned."*

Jesus is stating the law of seedtime, growth time and harvest time. All is recorded in heavenly courts. Our own words will be used to determine our fate. On the other hand, we can remain in covenant with God. When our soul-hearts are filled with God's words, we choose life-giving words and actions. As it is stated in Hosea 10:12-13

> *12Sow for yourselves righteousness; Reap in mercy; Break up your fallow ground, For it is time to seek the LORD, Till He comes and rains righteousness on you. 13You have plowed wickedness; You have reaped iniquity. You have eaten the fruit of lies, Because you trusted in your own way, In the multitude of your mighty men.*

Our fallow ground is our soul. What we plant there produces our actions and words. God gives us a free will to choose. Believers have chosen to function within God's righteousness. As creator, God designed how this creation would function. It is His work and His rules. The principle of seedtime, growth time and harvest time records our actions and words harvesting either blessings from God or permanent separation.

Think and write about it

1. How does God maintain the presence of His righteousness in the earthly realm?

2. How do our own words help keep us in God's covenant?

3. In your own words, describe how the principle of seedtime, growth time and harvest time functions in our earthly realm.

A fourth principle of the Kingdom of God is related to the third. Our Creator God possesses all He created. God chooses to share ownership and responsibility with His created human family. As noted, it is to be an intimate, mutual relationship. In covenant, each member gives something to the other. We, His people, give praise and worship. We surrender our wills and lives to algin with His purposes for His creation. The fourth principle is an act we can complete that demonstrates giving honor to

God. It is tithing. When we give God the first ten percent of our labor, we are reminding ourselves and God that He is first place in all our work. It is an act of our will to surrender something of value to us. God taught this principle to Adam in the garden. Abraham completed it in love. Moses recorded it as a commandment. Jesus discussed it as a heart issue with His disciples (Luke 6:38).

Returning to Genesis chapters one and two, we find the earliest instruction from Father God for functioning within the Kingdom of God principles. As noted earlier, after creating Adam, God placed him in the Garden of Eden with specific instructions. One of the first instructions concentrates on obeying and trusting God. One tree out of many was denied Adam. Or one could say God chose one tree for His own and then gave all the others to Adam. As recorded in Genesis 2:16 – 17:

> *And the LORD God commanded the man, saying, "Of every tree of the garden you may freely eat; [17]but of the tree of the knowledge of good and evil you shall not eat, for in the day that you eat of it you shall surely die."*

Commanded means a rule decreed. God gave abundantly to Adam. Only one tree of many trees remained God's possession. In one manner, this is to be the first tithe offering of humanity. To honor the relationship with God, He told Adam to give Him one tree. Not only is this an act of obedience, but also a daily offering to God. What is meant in this transaction is that life is maintained in the proper order of God's Kingdom principles when humanity offers some of His possessions back to God. This principle is found throughout God's word. The most notable promises of life tied to offering is Malachi 3:10 -11.

> [10]*Bring all the tithes into the storehouse, That there may be food in My house, And try Me now in this," Says the LORD of hosts, "If I will not open for you the windows of heaven And pour out for you such blessing That there will not be room enough to receive it. [11]And I will rebuke the devourer for your sakes, So that he will not destroy the fruit of your ground, Nor shall the vine fail to bear fruit for you in the field," Says the LORD of hosts...*

God even invites His people to test this Kingdom principle by doing what is required. So the fourth principle of God's Kingdom is making tithes and offerings to God that honor Him. This action will bring life to the believer. In addition, God will exercise His authority when His people honor Him this way by rebuking the destroyer. A guard will be placed around the rest of the people's possessions when they willingly follow this Kingdom principle.

Jesus clarifies the intent of this Kingdom of God principle of tithing in Luke 6:38 when describing acceptable practices of a believer.

Give, and it will be given to you: good measure, pressed down, shaken together, and running over will be put into your bosom. For with the same measure that you use, it will be measured back to you."

Now the soul-heart's intent is added to the honoring of God in surrendering a portion of what has been given by God to a person. The action of honoring God is not to be a religious habit. It is not simply an arrangement or deal with God. Jesus makes it clear, the attitude of the heart-soul, or measure is recorded by God. To give at this level of understanding is an act of love. Paul expands this in his instructions with the Corinthians in 2 Corinthians 9: 6 – 7

6But this I say: He who sows sparingly will also reap sparingly, and he who sows bountifully will also reap bountifully. 7So let each one give as he purposes in his heart, not grudgingly or of necessity; for God loves a cheerful giver.

Paul makes clear God's intent in giving. If we summarize all these passages, we know God's greater purposes in teaching us to give. The believer is to reach out and give to grow a cheerful heart. By honoring God's principle of tithing and giving in love, we become like our God. We are to be generous to reflect the heart of our God, trusting God to provide for all our needs. It is an act of faith out of love for God. This is the fourth Kingdom of God principle of tithing. As in all of them we are to become the children of God and reflect on earth the truth of the Kingdom of God.

Think and Write about it

How does God use tithes and offerings to teach His people to be like Jesus Christ?

8

Operating within Kingdom of God Principles

Entering Deeper in Spiritual Realms

The Bible is the source for learning the Kingdom of God principles. There are layers of understanding and wisdom written into all the words. The writings of the books of the Bible are under the direction of The Holy Spirit (2 Timothy 3:16 – 17). Since these words come directly from God, they are full of life. It is for this reason it is necessary the words be approached through one's spirit body. For what is eternal requires spiritual ears and eyes to know, not soul eyes and ears which were clouded by the world's view of wisdom. Jesus declared this truth of the spirit when He tried to explain His role as the bread of life. As recorded in John 6:63

> *It is the Spirit who gives life; the flesh profits nothing. The words that I speak to you are spirit, and they are life.*

This is what Jesus was conveying to the people. Spirit-to-spirit communication will give life to the believer. Knowing in the flesh bodies is what the Pharisees were accused of doing as they read and interpreted scriptures, increasing the rules based on man's wisdom (Matthew 23:13 -22). As Jesus stated to them this produces nothing in the Kingdom of God. As noted in earlier chapters, spirit-to-spirit communication is achieved through faith in action.

As outlined in earlier chapters, a believer is to enter the relationship with Father God as a child, willing to learn. The soul-heart is to be cleansed of the world's understanding so the spirit body may dwell deeper within the person. A habit of approaching God from the Holy Spirit, through one's spirit body, then soul body, and finally flesh body develops as the old soul-heart is crucified. When this occurs, the multiple levels of revelation within the Bible now can enter the spirit body and imprint spiritual truth on the soul-heart. As this happens, the words of the Bible, which are alive in the spirit, align the surrendered three bodies to the principles of the Kingdom of God.

Entering the spiritual realm requires faith and surrender to Jesus Christ as Lord and all He has accomplished. This faith is the mustard seed of faith. It is to grow and be planted in the spiritual realm. Old seeds of habits attempt to choke out this seed of faith. They lie fallow within the soul-heart. As Jesus stated in the parable of the seed, faith that grows near the old seeds can strangle this faith with the cares of the world (Mathew 13: 1- 9). Stresses in life can harden soul-hearts. Doublemindedness can grow with loyalties divided between King Jesus and people or organizations. If a person does not learn how to align the three bodies with the will of God, these conditions of the soul-heart and soul-mind may not be noticed. The old seeds grow slowly, pulling the faith-focused soul-heart and soul-mind into brambles of time spent on world-driven emergencies (Luke 8:14). The old seeds grow and call a person to revert to the way they solved life issues before accepting Jesus Christ as Lord. Our covenant with the blood of Jesus is a commitment to the will of God being made known in the earthly realm. We are to live in our spirits while functioning in our physical bodies. Alignment is to be checked daily. We are to recognize when we are off balance so we can return to proper relationship of dependency on King Jesus. If we fail to notice the pulling of old habits and attitudes or forms of coping, we attempt to understand God's word with polluted soul-hearts. This weighs down the soul body to an earthly focus and limits access to spiritual truth. God is holy. He calls those who enter His presence to cleanse themselves and be holy as He is holy. If a person chooses to seek God with one's whole heart, the Holy Spirit will convict one of this crooked alignment within the three bodies. Learning to operate in the spiritual realm within balanced three bodies allows a person to function in greater consciousness in the spiritual realm. As a person surrenders to the will of God in the spiritual realm, greater intimacy with God occurs. With this intimacy comes greater revelation within spiritual truths.

Applying Basic Kingdom of God Principles

Father God continues to teach His creation. He is alive and active in the lives of the people who willing seek Him. As with our own parental relationships, we are instructed and led by God (Hebrews 12:5 – 7). Father God taught Adam Kingdom principles when he lived in the Garden of Eden. As noted in an earlier chapter, by tending the garden, Adam learned about seedtime, growth time and harvest time. There is a flow to life or rhythm starting in heaven and coming spiritually into the earthly realm. What is seen and known in the earthly realm is a physical image of its origin in the spiritual realm. Within our earth seasons, day and night, and atmospheric conditions combine to nurture seed growth. This unity of multiple elements allows what is planted to grow to optimum results. As Adam tended this garden and listened to the rhythm and unity of the plants with their environment, he heard a dependency for life coming from heaven. He also learned to seek and honor patterns within the spiritual realm. These were to be repeated in the earthly realm in order to maintain life as it was created. His spirit ears and eyes allowed Adam to know harmony began in the spiritual realm and the created world responded to it. John records this understanding in John 1:1 - 4

> *¹In the beginning was the Word, and the Word was with God, and the Word was God. ²He was in the beginning with God. ³All things were made through Him, and without Him nothing was made that was made. ⁴In Him was life, and the life was the light of men.*

Since our God has always been three-in-one, Adam would have known all three forms of God. The bond between harmony with the spiritual realm and life on earth was clear to Adam. To maintain life, one is to remain in harmony with the Word of God. We on the other side of the cross, know Jesus Christ is the Word incarnate. Learning the rhythm and harmony of the Kingdom of God today is knowing Jesus Christ, who is the source of all life. Thus, this Kingdom Principle is to live in harmony with Jesus Christ in all His ways to maintain life.

As Adam tended the plants, he learned another Kingdom of God principle called seedtime, growth time and harvest time. What is planted in the earth, or released in the ground, produces after its own kind. There is a necessary growth time between planting and harvest. Environmental conditions as well as availability of necessary resources for growth effect the amount of harvest. Life during the "time" is directly proportional to how the ground and seeds are cultivated. God is teaching His people that it is not simply the planting of seeds that affect the harvest, but also what is done in between.

Since humanity is created in the likeness of God, what we say with our mouths creates in the spiritual realm. God spoke the world into existence. We also create with all our words. We literally plant words that create seeds within the spiritual realm. Jesus explained this Kingdom of God principle to the people in Matthew 12:35 - 37

> *35A good man out of the good treasure of his heart brings forth good things, and an evil man out of the evil treasure brings forth evil things. 36But I say to you that for every idle word men may speak, they will give account of it in the day of judgment. 37For by your words you will be justified, and by your words you will be condemned."*

The heart Jesus is speaking about is the soul-heart, not the physical heart. Soul consists of spiritual substances. What comes from the spirit plants within the spiritual realm. As Adam learned, what is planted grows and develops a fruit, and produces multiple seeds. There is a harvest for what people create during their time of living in the earthly realm. Words are alive in the spiritual realm. They are planted and grow. What we do to feed and support them during their growth time effects the harvest. Evil hearts produce a crop of seeds that are filled with rebellion and chaos. Continually planting and feeding these types of seeds brings destruction into the person's life. God created a way to eradicate destructive seeds, ending a bad harvest. When we surrender our lives and call upon God, He can intervene with the seeds we planted. This is the function of repentance, confession, and forgiveness. Now, on this side of the cross, the method of destroying evil seeds is accepting Jesus Christ as Lord of one's life. As described in an earlier chapter, this is not simply stating words. It is a daily surrender of the old way of living, cleansing out the soul-heart with confession, repentance and applying the blood of Jesus. It is seeking King Jesus in a personal, intimate relationship.

A cleansed good heart needs to be maintained and fed to continually grow and be productive in the spiritual realm. We have an active enemy attempting to help us plant destructive seeds. As stated in 1 Peter 5:8 – 9:

> *8Be sober, be vigilant; because your adversary the devil walks about like a roaring lion, seeking whom he may devour. 9Resist him, steadfast in the faith, knowing that the same sufferings are experienced by your brotherhood in the world.*

Activating faith daily in our God keeps us awake and alert in the spiritual realm. It allows us to guard what is planted and to rip up destructive seeds. We nurture good new seeds through practicing the tools Jesus Christ gave us to align with Kingdom of God principles.

Just as Adam learned, tending a good plant takes work. Tending our soul-hearts takes time and effort. It is working one's faith. Anything that is planted in the spirit realm is alive. Our soul bodies are spiritual. When believers declare God's truths and write them on their soul-hearts, they are aligning themselves with the Kingdom of God principles. Life is in the word of God. Declaring the word and owning it as truth for oneself feeds good seeds. It also creates willing soil within the soul body to plant more words of God's truth. This action of faith is aligning with the harmony coming from the spiritual realm. A rhythm to the pattern in the spirit realm can now be discerned as a person applies this continual faith action in one's daily life.

Think and Write about it:

What are the two Kingdom of God principles that Adam was taught through tending plants?

As mentioned in an earlier chapter, Father God taught Adam to seek in the spiritual realm for the truth God embedded in animals. Action is required for applying the Kingdom of God principles in this learning. We, God's children are to seek God's truth with the spiritual organs of our spiritual bodies when operating within this earthly realm. Our starting point is to be within our awakened spiritual bodies, not our physical bodies. Our references are to be on spiritual truths not the manifestations in the physical world. These truths have been written on our soul bodies when we have eaten and meditated on God's words. God honored Abraham by declaring him righteous for believing God (Romans 4:3). Abraham trusted in the word of God over what was natural in the earthly realm. He did not consider the problem as the physical world defines it. He kept his focus on God. As recorded in Romans 4:21-22

> *21...and being fully convinced that what He had promised He was also able to perform. 22And therefore "it was accounted to him for righteousness."*

His obedience and hope led to pulling what God had declared into the earthly realm from the spiritual realm. It is what Father God was teaching Adam to do by seeing into the spiritual and declaring in the earthly realm the true nature of animals. Abraham stood on the faith that God would accomplish all God said He would. Trust is in God for who He is, not simply what He promised. Abraham applied his faith and trust in God to call what was true in the spiritual realm into his life, despite what the physical realm demonstrated as truth. His wife would conceive despite evidence of a shrunken womb. God would raise his son Isaac, even though he was to be sacrificed. As it is recorded in Romans 4:17 – 18:

> *17...(as it is written, " I have made you a father of many nations") in the presence of Him whom he believed— God, who gives life to the dead and calls those things which do not exist as though they did; 18who, contrary to hope, in hope believed, so that he became the father of many nations, according to what was spoken, " So shall your descendants be."*

We are the descendants of Abraham through our faith, not a physical bloodline. We are to call that which we "see" in the spiritual realm into the earthly realm. This is how the Kingdom of God is manifested in the earthly realm. To "see" in the spirit, we are to first know what we are seeking by having written it on our soul bodies. We are to call the perfect into the imperfect. To accomplish this task, we are to function in the spiritual realm while living in the physical realm.

Think and Write about it:

1. What are the similarities between the method of naming animals God taught Adam and what Abraham did in faith?

2. Which principle of the Kingdom of God did Abraham demonstrate in faith?

Learning to Operate in the Spiritual Realm

To achieve the task of functioning in the spirit, we are to start with our faith in Jesus Christ as Lord. Obedience to God's words is the pathway to expressing faith (John 14:15). After cleansing the soul-heart of the old ways, we create a new compass for our soul-hearts. This takes time and working with the Holy Spirit. Habits that are formed as we seek an intimate relationship with God and build an avenue in our spirit bodies to find God in the spirit realm. Praise is one of the avenues that gives quick access to our God. As stated in Psalm 22:3:

> *But You are holy, Enthroned in the praises of Israel.*

As we praise our God and focus on Him, we enter our spiritual bodies. Here we let go of our own concerns and seek only to honor God. God hears our soul-heart intents and answers by inhabiting our praises. In these moments our spiritual ears and eyes are opened in greater measure. We can now listen and sense God's presence in greater depth. The more we practice this action the greater our spiritual eyes and ears will open. Remember it is to be done in surrender, not through selfish motives. God can discern our soul-hearts intents and will not be drawn to praise that is not soul-heart centered in honoring God.

Another way of opening spiritual organs within one's spiritual body is through the habits formed in a personal prayer closet. In prayer closets, we ask Holy Spirit to reveal God's words at a new level. Then we listen. Just like we heard convictions of trespasses and other forms of rebellion from the Holy Spirit when crucifying the old soul-heart, now we listen for wisdom. This is truly a rising up into the spirit body and letting go of self-focus. Speaking in tongues will expedite moving from the soul body focus into the spirit body centering. Combining reading the word of God with speaking in tongues facilitates the opening of spiritual truths in the word of God. It is an active way of trusting Holy Spirit to lead, rather than leaning into one's own wisdom. We are to bind these revealed Biblical truths to our soul bodies so we can recognize them when we again enter the spiritual realm in our spiritual bodies. The spiritual truths have form in the spiritual realm. They are full of life and move in this realm. Familiarity with these truths allows a person to perceive them. This is why it is important to write Biblical spiritual truths revealed through meditating on God's words on our soul-hearts.

When a person has awakened the spiritual organs, it is possible to consciously know in the spiritual realm. Each time one chooses to enter the spiritual realm, an active surrender to our triune God is declared. It is a letting go of soul body, centering into spirit body focus. It is done in faith and trusting who King Jesus is. He is the door, the way, and the truth. No one can enter except through Him. Declare:

> ➢ I surrender my heart, my mind, and my will to you, Father God.
>
> ➢ I surrender my heart, my mind, and my will to you, Jesus Christ.
>
> ➢ I surrender my heart, my mind and my will to you, Holy Spirit.
>
> ➢ Fill me with your presence God.

Then enter into praise to our God for who He is. Name some of God's attributes you know very well. Let go of any control or need and rise into your spirit body. Just rest in God's presence, not expecting anything to happen. Remove the limitations of the soul-mind that judges and expects results. Truly rest in timelessness. Float in your spirit body in God's peace and wait. The spiritual truths you have bonded to your soul-heart will attract similar truths in the spiritual realm. Like draws to like. Listen with your spiritual ears and look with your spiritual eyes. It is now up to the Holy Spirit to lead. Sometimes it is just to spend quality time in the presence of God. Other times, wisdom is given. Sometimes, the Holy Spirit will lead you to call forth what is sensed around you. Declare it out loud as you are led. When you sense a drawing back of the Spirit, and a different peace comes into you, it is an indicator the time is over. Return to soul body by praising and honoring God for what He has shared with you. All good things come from God, and we are to acknowledge this in praise.

In this communion with God, we may be led to declare what God wants into our earthly regions. It is calling what is not as if it were already done here in the earthly realm. God's words are what we release in the space we shared with Him in the spiritual realm. When we have bonded the fruits of the spirit to our soul hearts, we recognize them in the spiritual realm (Galatians 5:22 – 23). We may be asked to call these forth. Holy Spirit may lead some to call physical body parts that are perfect into the imperfect bodies of those whom we are bringing to God for healing. Others may be led to call weapons of warfare from the spiritual to align the imperfect into God's perfect will in various circumstances. Some are called to release the same power of God at an earlier event in Biblical history. We can bring power from these events into present situations. The caller has an intimate understanding of the layers of revelation in these events and recognizes them being offered in God's Glory. In remembrance of them, the power of God can be released by those called to declare them. In each case, it is aligning the imperfect earthly situation to the perfect one found in the Kingdom of God. Always the one being led to call God's will into a situation has developed an intimate wisdom of what is being asked to enter from the spiritual realm. This knowing within a person is alive in one's spirit. It is achieved through in-depth study of the living word of God.

The Holy Spirit directs those who are seeking the face of God in the process of preparation. Time spent in prayer closets and time spent meditating on words of God build foundations to write the spiritual truths on soul-hearts. There are no quick fixes in building these foundations. These building blocks are teaching the person to align all three personal bodies to the perfect will of God. Each one of us is the temple of God. Before we can truly surrender them to God, the spirit body must guide and lead the other two bodies into alignment. This alignment is done in winning the battle over past understanding that is contrary God's words. It is tearing down double-minded belief systems that honor anything as having equal value to God. It is subjugating any emotional ties within earthly desires to the will of God. Alignment requires listening to the Holy Spirit to find any vestiges left from the spirit of religion and destroying them. This alignment process requires searching for anything left from structures of guilt, shame, blame, offense, bitterness and unforgiveness, and tearing them out by the roots. Everything in thoughts, emotions, beliefs, and attitudes are to be examined and aligned with the will of God. Once a person achieves alignment, it must be practiced on a daily basis as events in life occur. These daily actions give the believer clean hands and a clean heart so the believer may be intimate with God. Now we are walking in the faith of Father Abraham! In this state we can call what is not in this imperfect world from the spiritual realm into existence through our faith.

As mentioned in earlier chapters, God gives us the right and responsibility to release His will into our earthly realm. He also calls us to bind His will into this earthly realm. Critical to this process are two things. The first is to know God's will. Again, the alignment process described above is essential to knowing God's will and recognizing it. Praise and prayer are the vehicles to knowing God's will in each situation. Through praise we enter correct relationship with God. We submit to God's authority. Declaring our relationship to His authority and using Bible verses in praise allows the three bodies to algin with God at that particular moment. Even in corporate worship, individuals are responsible to engage in praise. For it is in praise that God inhabits the presence of His people. Only with the right attitude toward our God may we complete what is recorded in Philippians 4:6

> *Be anxious for nothing, but in everything by prayer and supplication, with thanksgiving, let your requests be made known to God;*

We seek God's will. Honor and authority are in God. When we request His attention, it is with our individual faith we have surrendered to God.

The second part of the process is how we use the loosing and binding principles within the protocol of the courts of heaven. Then we are to embrace who we are in Jesus Christ. Stay under the covenant of the Blood of Jesus! This will include actions and words which we are to loose from the heavenly realm. It is one of the forms of spiritual warfare. We may loose the blood of Jesus from the mercy seat to overcome a situation. This is one of many weapons. Having entered God's presence we have listened for His directions and what He tells us to loose. It is not something that starts from our soul-minds but rather from our spirit bodies. We are listening spirit-to-spirit for directions. Are we to bind the fruits of the Spirit to our situations? For example, we can call the peace of God to bind to soul-hearts. Recall how David instructed his own soul. He called this through declaring who God is and his relationship to God (Psalm 42). Sometimes while functioning in the will of God, He instructs us to bind His attributes to others as a covering. Other times it is to pour and bind that attribute from the Holy Spirit, through their spirits, then souls and then to their physical bodies. We may bind the light of God to a person to overcome the darkness within them and drive it out. We are to stay within our authority and alignment with the courts of heaven. We are given power and authority over the enemy when we operate within the covenant of the blood of Jesus. When we stand in judgment, we are outside of the covenant. We do not have the right or authority to judge. When Jesus cleansed the demoniac, He loosed the man from the demons and sent them into the pigs (Matthew 8:28-34). He did not bind them. He did not bind and send the demons to hell. We are to be in Jesus Christ's likeness. It is the risen King Jesus who has the keys to hell, grave, and death. He opens and locks these doors; we do not. As believers operate in these Kingdom of God principles, it is best to follow a simple rule. When dealing with individuals bind what is good and pure and holy to people and separate what is of the enemy from people and situations. After removing the enemy's effects, then bind the goodness of God to them!

Remember what John teaches us in 1 John 2:27:

> *But the anointing which you have received from Him abides in you, and you do not need that anyone teach you; but as the same anointing teaches you concerning all things, and is true, and is not a lie, and just as it has taught you, you will abide in Him.*

Abide in God. Abide is resting completely in God's peace. We who obey the commands of King Jesus have the promise of not only Jesus Christ living in us, but also God the Father and the Holy Spirit. They live in us through Jesus Christ. We also live in them. Through the baptism of the Holy Spirit the anointing instructs us on how to accomplish all this. Seek God and His Kingdom and He will be found. Do not stop loving and wanting more of God. He is pleased with those who keep seeking His face. Holy Spirit will lead all those who have this desire and love into a deeper relationship with God. In that relationship, the words of God will come alive in each believer.

Become mature sons and daughters of God as was intended when you entered this earthly realm.

Think and Write about it:

1. What are the basic steps believers follow when seeking God's intervention in their lives?

2. How do we apply our faith like Father Abraham to earthly situations?

3. What do we have the authority to loose and bind in the earthly realm?

References

Thomas Nelson: NKJV. Holy Bible. Thomas Nelson. Kindle Edition

Thomas Nelson: NIV. Holy Bible. Thomas Nelson. Kindle Edition

Vine, W. E. Vines, Unger, Merrill, & White Jr. William. <u>Complete Repository Dictionary</u>. (Thomas Nelson Publishers) 1996.

Blue Letter Bible.org. Publishers the BLB Institute. Online application

Author's Website
dianeneumann.com

Additional Books by Author
Available in paperback or eBook format

At Advantage Books

God's Resting Place. 2025

Freedom within the Kingdom of God. 2025

At Amazon

Weapons of Praise. 2020

The Power of Discipleship. 2020

Seeking God's Righteousness. 2021

Covenant: A Relationship Between Two Kingdoms. 2021

Grace: An Attribute of God. 2022

Breaking Chains Through the Power of Christ Jesus. 2021

Author Biography

Diane Neumann is a retired educator, having worked in grades 1-14. She served as a teacher, counselor, administrator, and staff developer. Diane is a certified minister under the authority of Church Growth International of the Americas. In ministry she served 16 years as a spiritual mentor working with men and women seeking a Christian solution to addictions. For the last five years, the Holy Spirit has been leading her to write and complete books to help people who are seeking a closer walk with God.

OTHER BOOKS BY DIANE M. NEUMANN:
Freedom Within the Kingdom of God
God's Resting Place

COMING SOON:
Authority of the Blood of Jesus

FOR MORE INFORMATION CONTACT ADVANTAGE BOOKS:
info@advbooks.com

Advantage
BOOKS

Advantage Books
Orlando, Florida
we bring dreams to life